How to Make Money in the Guitar Biz

Turn Your Passion into a Profession

By Alan Morrison

Copyright 2014

John,
Welcome to the
"Guitar Biz"!

Alan Morrison

This book is dedicated to my lovely wife, Julie, who has always encouraged me to follow my dreams. Also, to my kids Nick and Brianna who have both played a part in the dream. Thank you to my parents who taught me about hard work and keeping the faith. Thank you to my customers who have helped AM Guitar Works grow through their continued support and referrals.

Thank you to...

Dan Downing, who invited me to teach guitar at Moore Music while in college.

Arlen Ottmar, who hired me as a technician/guitar instructor/retail salesperson at Ottmar Music.

Bentwood - Doug, Jim, and Mike who I had the pleasure of playing music with for 13 years.

The Wedding Singers – Dave and Carrie – you guys rock!

Identity Crisis – current and former members - Dave, Dino, Drew, Eric, Jason,Jim, John, Kathy, Kris, Mike, Nicole, Pat, Roy, Shauna, Terry, Tom B, and Tom S. You are a talented, fun group of people to make music with.

Cover Design by: Mike Shield - Shield Design

Cover Photography by: Brianna Morrison - Breezy Rae Photography

Proofreading: Chelsea Morrison

Final Editing by: Ann and John Valus

Foreword

"Guitar players are a dime a dozen".

I'll always remember hearing that from a fellow guitar player many years ago. Not meaning to cheapen the value of guitar players, he merely meant that there are LOTS of them. Everyone wants to play the guitar. That's good news for you.

I met Alan Morrison in an intermediate school band room in 2004 when we were forming our cover band, "Identity Crisis" (www.IdentityCrisisQCA.com). Alan had a long career going as a regional service manager for a national office equipment company. He was also a talented guitarist and tinkerer, having experience in electronics repair and adjusting guitars. He always played a red Fender Strat, but one night he showed up with a blue one. He proudly said that he built it, pointing out the "AM Guitars" logo on the headstock. (To this day, that blue guitar is his go-to axe present at every gig).

From here, Alan began taking on guitar setup and repair work on a bench in his basement. Each time I went to his house, there were a few more guitars, tools, etc. I was doing work in IT at the time, and Alan asked me to help him set up a web site. I spent a couple of hours with him getting his domain registered, and I got him started with web authoring and how to FTP files to his site. I anticipated phone calls and return visits, but I never heard from him again – he figured it all out himself, including setting up his online store for parts. In other words, he's a pretty smart guy. At some point he expressed a desire to do this full time someday.

On a cold December night at a music concert, Alan walked up with a big smile and said, "I quit my job today – they were stunned!" I'm sure they were. Alan, the consummate straight arrow, is anything but a risk-taker, yet he walked away from a solid job with benefits to pursue his dream.

It wasn't long before Alan was able to move out of his basement and into a small shop, then a larger shop, and then into a nice retail space in a great location. He has steadily expanded his products and services, including classes in which students build guitars, amplifiers and effects. He has a loyal following, including me – I won't let anyone else work on my guitars.

This book should be very helpful for anyone who would like to start from scratch and begin to make money in the guitar business. Consider yourself lucky that Alan has chosen to share his methods for success.

As Alan likes to say, "stay tuned…."

John Korn

Table of Contents

Introduction

"How To Make Money In the Guitar Biz" is exactly what the title says. It is good information that you will find useful whether you are looking to make a little extra money on the side, or whether you are considering making the guitar a full time business venture. Maybe you already own a guitar business and are looking for new ideas. There are also strategies in this book that can apply to ANY small business whether it is guitar related or not.

"How To Make Money In the Guitar Biz" is not a "get rich quick" book. It's not even a "get rich" book. This book is based on my experiences at making money with guitars. I also interviewed others in the guitar biz including professional touring musicians, a lesson studio owner, and some guitar builders. I am a small business owner and entrepreneur. Owning a successful small business and watching it grow is one of the most satisfying things a person can do, especially if it involves doing something you love.

The book will give a little of my personal background, then talk about how AM Guitar Works started and has continued to grow and evolve from a part time to full time home based business to moving into a commercial retail space. I will discuss in detail the facets of the business and strategies used to market and grow the business.

Now let's get started Making Money in the Guitar Biz!

Chapter 1
Where it All Began

I grew up on a farm in southwest Iowa. When I was around 9 years old, we got a nylon string guitar from the Green Stamp Store. I learned to play a few chords on it. At age 12 I got my first electric guitar – a used Sears Silvertone. It was a model built by Danelectro in the 60's with the tube amplifier built into the case. I paid $35 for it and sold it a few years later for $50 thinking I came out ahead. Now those guitars are selling for 10 times what I paid for it. The nearest guitar teacher was 30 miles away, so for the most part, I learned on my own.

My father was a farmer, carpenter, and also owned a TV repair shop. So I grew up around hard work, woodworking, electronics and small business.

During my high school years (in the late 70's and early 80's) I was forming bands and jamming with friends. I would also spend hours looking at Allparts, Mighty Mite, Warmoth, Stewart MacDonald and many other guitar part and tool catalogs thinking about what guitars I could build with those parts if I only had the money. I subscribed to *Guitar Player* magazine and read every issue cover to cover, learning about the trends, technology and terminology.

In high school, I removed the bolt-on neck from a damaged Epiphone 12 string acoustic guitar. I bought some birdseye maple and had a woodworker cut out a body shape that I designed. My dad helped with the routing and other finer woodworking parts. I put it all together and installed the electronics. That was my start in tinkering with guitars.

At the same time I was honing my skills as a guitarist. As a teen growing up in the 70's, there was a lot of cool guitar music going on. I would come home from school, go up to my room and learn my favorite songs, eat supper, then head back up to my room to play more guitar. I didn't consider it practice, I was just playing music.

Growing up around a TV shop also gave me some experience with electronics. I took an electronics correspondence course during high school. After high school, I went to Southwestern Community College in Creston, IA. I earned an Associate's degree in Electronics Technology. I figured this would help me work on amplifiers.

During my college years, a music store manager asked me if I would like to give guitar lessons at their store. At that time lessons were $4 per half hour. I was making $8 per hour at a time when minimum wage was $3.35. I found this to be easy money for a college student.

I also ended up playing in a couple bands as well. This gave me experience in performing for money.

I was going to electronics school, teaching guitar lessons, and playing in bands. Although it was a dream at the time, these things helped lead to the point where I am today - making money in the guitar biz!

Upon graduation from electronics school, I went to work for an office equipment company as a service technician. It was in the same town as the music store, so I continued giving guitar lessons and playing in the band on weekends. Looking back, I've spent most of my life using my music-related talents and skills to earn extra money.

After a year of the office equipment business, I responded to an ad in the newspaper for a repair technician at Ottmar Music Center in Atlantic, IA. I applied, and got the job, and moved to Atlantic. I repaired guitars, amplifiers, stereo equipment, organs, and sound equipment. We serviced all makes and models of equipment, which taught me how to be versatile. I also gave guitar lessons and was in charge of guitar and sound equipment sales. I learned some sales techniques from this experience. I also learned about the inner workings of a music store, such as inventory management, retail strategies, and more.

At this time I joined an established band, Bentwood, from nearby Adair, IA. It was while living in Atlantic that I met Julie, the love of my life. I saved up enough band money to pay cash for an engagement ring. I loved the music store job, but it was not paying enough for a newly married couple. I ended up getting back into the office equipment business and we moved to Des Moines. Even though it was a longer drive, I still played in the band.

After about 12 years in the Des Moines area, I was promoted to a management position in Davenport, IA. Davenport is 175 miles east of Des Moines and the band I was based in was another hour west. One of the hardest things about this decision was leaving the band. We had been together for 13 years by this time, 13 years of playing gigs with the same 4 guys. We'd been through members getting married, having kids and some really good times. It was what I had to do though, to better myself financially. It turned out that Davenport was a good place for me to go. It ended up being the land of opportunity for me to "make money in the guitar biz".

Shortly after moving to Davenport, a family friend asked if I would give his daughter guitar lessons. At the time I had my eye on a Fender American Deluxe Stratocaster. I figured giving some lessons would help pay for the Strat. Pretty soon I had three students, then six, then 10, then 15…. I was making money in the guitar biz! I was also playing in a band and subbing wherever I could. I started playing guitar and bass at my church as well.

In 2004, I was called upon to play for a local theatre musical production because I was a guitarist who could actually read music. It was during this musical that I got to know the drummer, Terry Reiter, who was also my son's drum instructor and 7th grade band director. Terry told me he would like to start a classic rock band with a horn section. He was looking for a guitarist. I thought that sounded like fun – and it is. There are 12 people on stage and a sound engineer. Many of the members are band and orchestra directors, private instructors, or just veteran rockers who have played in bands for years. Besides being lots of fun, it has been a great way to network. I currently do lots of business with the schools because many of the local band directors know me.

This brings me to the start of my small business, which was originally named AM Guitar Repair. More details on this later in the book. To make a long story short – I started repairing guitars for students and friends. With some networking and a website launch, within a year I had enough work to go full time into the guitar business – first as a home-based business, then in commercial retail space. This is my background and leads up to the point where I am at today.

Next each chapter will discuss the different ways that money can be made in the guitar biz in detail. You will learn about the many income opportunities and strategies that I use. I will also discuss strategies that can apply to *any* small business.

Feel free to recommend this book to any of your friends who are either small business owners, or would like to be someday.

Let's look at a very basic 4 step business strategy.

Basic Business Strategy #1
1. Create a product or offer a service
2. Find customers who are willing to pay for your product or service
3. Keep the customers coming back and get them to refer others
4. Network to grow the business

This is a strategy I have used repeatedly to grow and expand the business. It's not a one-time instant success formula. You can continually start at step one by adding new products and services. We'll use this four step strategy throughout the book and discuss in details, the steps you can take to succeed in these areas.

Chapter 2

Lessons

This chapter will discuss making money in the guitar biz by giving lessons. This chapter could apply to any musical instrument lessons as well. In my opinion, this is an easy way to make money. There is no investment required. All you need is some time and space to give lessons. It is easily done out of your home. You can also teach at music stores or lesson studios as well.

When you know how to do something that others don't and are willing to teach them, there is money to be made.

So, how do you get students? Lots of people want to learn to play guitar – young and old. My current students range in age from 7 to 70. You just have to let those people find you.

My first experience with teaching guitar started at Moore Music in Creston, IA while I was in college. The store provided me with students and I got to keep all the money. All I had to do was keep students and parents coming into the store once a week, sell books and tell them when they were ready to upgrade to a new guitar.

These days, most music stores will let you rent lesson studio space for a few dollars per lesson. In some areas there are dedicated music lesson studios that operate the same way.

You can also teach out of your home and save the rental fee, but you will have to find your own students.

Here are a list of pros and cons of teaching from home versus renting studio space.

Music Store or Lesson Studio

Pros:

- *Students will be provided (check with music store)*
- *You have a professional teaching environment*
- *You do not have people coming through your home every half hour*

Cons:

- *You have to pay for the use of studio time*
- *It takes time away from home*
- *Travel expense to and from the studio*
- *If you have time gaps between students you are away from home*

Teaching from Home

Pros:

- *You don't have to pay for studio time*
- *No travel time and expense to studio*
- *You are home and can spend time with family or doing "home things" during time gaps between lessons*
- *You can deduct a percentage of your rent/mortgage payment and utilities on your taxes when you run a home based business*

Cons:

- *You are responsible for finding your own students*
- *You will have people coming through your home every hour or half hour*

Once you've decided when and where you are going to teach, you are on step one of Business Strategy #1 Decide on a product or service.

Now we are on step 2. Find people who are willing to pay for your product or service. So, how do you get students? Even if you teach from a music store or lesson studio, you don't want to count on them to provide you with every student. The best way I have found is simple networking. Start with your family and friends. They may already know that you play guitar and would be willing to let you teach them or their kids.

The majority of my guitar students start when they are in middle school or early high school. When kids hit that age, they are starting to figure out who they are. They are starting to decide what kind of music they like and want to learn. They don't have their driver's license or are not busy with jobs or girlfriends and boyfriends yet. They have time to practice their instrument and develop their skills. It makes the parents feel better about paying for guitar lessons when they hear their son or daughter practicing or playing songs.

Make an effort to introduce yourself and get to know your middle school and high school band, orchestra, and music teachers. I've gotten lots or referrals from teachers. It helped that my children were in their classes. My kids would also let their friends know that I taught guitar. There's no shame in having your kids refer business to you. Some schools have lists of private music instructors so that when kids or parents ask, they refer to someone on the list. Contact your local schools and ask to be on the list. If you don't have kids in school, attend a band concert and introduce yourself to a director. Give them a business card.

If you attend church, see if there is a bulletin board where you can put up a poster or business card. I play guitar on a worship team at my church. Sometimes people walk up to me after a service and ask if I teach or know anyone who does. Several of my current students are members of my church. The more situations you put yourself in front of people playing guitar, the more people will think to come to you if they are looking for a guitar teacher.

It has been my experience that once you have a few students, you will start getting referrals. When kids start playing guitar, their friends want to play as well. That's when the referrals start rolling in.

Teaching Strategies
There are some various schools of thought on teaching lessons and I will cover them here. You have to teach based on your abilities and knowledge, but do not be afraid to expand your knowledge. Remember step 3 of Business Strategy #1 – Keep them coming back and referring others.

- Teaching Strategy 1 – Strictly "by the book"
- Teaching Strategy 2 – Throw the book out, skip the basics, teach songs or from your knowledge

- Teaching Strategy 3 – A combination of 1 and 2

Here is what I do. I teach out of a few different method books, depending on the student's age and previous music experience the student has had. I firmly believe in teaching the basics of reading music as it applies to guitar as well as teaching things that they want to learn to play. Because of my ability to read music there have been many more opportunities opened up to me. For each student I get, I require them to complete the first book of a guitar method. I tell them that when they complete that book, we will move on and play things that they want to learn. This gives them a goal to achieve. I always assign parts that they have to practice and play for the next lesson. I tell them the more they practice the faster we will get through the book and move on to other things. As we go through the book, I introduce them to simple songs that are not in the book as well to keep it interesting. In the first lesson, I try to teach a few chords and show them how to play at least part of a popular song so they leave their first lesson with something fun to practice.

Here are the books that I teach out of:

Hal Leonard Guitar For Kids
Hal Leonard FastTrack for Guitar Method Book 1
Guitar System Books 1,2&3 by Dana Starkell

I have had students who had previous guitar teachers that were using one of the first two strategies listed above and it caused them or their parents to get frustrated and leave that teacher.

Here is what happens with Teaching Strategy 1- Strictly "by the book". I had a student come to me who had been taking lessons for quite some time. His parents were looking for another teacher because he was obviously very talented, but not learning the songs he wanted to learn. He told me he was working out of a book. He was in method book 3. He had a great understanding of the basics, but was not able to play any of the songs he liked. I told him to put the book away. I pulled out the music to "Carry On Wayward Son" and started showing him how it was played. He and his parents walked away from his first lesson with me with big smiles on their faces. They felt like he learned more in one lesson with me than he had in a long time. The first instructor was good at giving him the basics, and a great foundation to build on. However, he was not moving on from there. He was just giving him more of the material that is in method books that no one really wants to play.

At the other end of the spectrum is the teacher who does not require a student to learn basics and goes right into trying to teach them their favorite song, usually using TAB notation. You end up with a student who is playing guitar by looking at lines and numbers. They may or may not have a clue what note they are playing. They are just looking at numbers. If someone puts a piece of music in front of them, they are unable to play it. This especially frustrates band directors. Johnny has been taking bass lessons for a couple years now and is asked to play for the high school jazz band. The director puts the music in front of him and he asks if he can get it in TAB. True story.

I am not saying that either way is wrong or that mine is the only right way to do it. What I am saying is that if you want to retain your students you need to challenge them and keep it interesting and fun at the same time. Also, if you are teaching kids, you need to keep the parents happy. They are the ones paying for the lessons. If their kids lose interest or aren't learning, you will lose them as students. All the business books will tell you it costs more money to gain new customers than to retain current customers. I have several students who have been with me for years.

I know there are lots of great guitarists out there who don't read music and there is nothing wrong with that. You may be one of them. If you want to teach guitar, however, I would highly recommend that you take yourself through a method book 1. It never hurts to learn new things.

You should also teach to your strengths. If you are an excellent fingerstyle guitarist or blues player, share your skills with your students. Help them expand their musical vocabulary.

Since this book is about making money, we should talk about what to charge and collecting payment. As far as what to charge, call around to see what others are charging for music lessons in your area. I have students pay for lessons a month at a time at the beginning of every month. I highly recommend this method of payment. That way the student is committed for at least a month. Also, if the student decides to stop showing up after 2 weeks, you still have the money.

I also highly recommend coming up with a policy document that you give your students explaining how you will handle cancellations, no-shows, and makeup lessons. Have the student or parents sign the document and keep it on file so both of you have a record of what was agreed to when they signed up for lessons. This makes it easier if there is a problem later on. Fortunately, I have not had the occasion to use this to enforce my policies, but it's a good idea to cover yourself and have your policies in writing. I call it a welcome letter, but it is really a signed agreement. At the end of this chapter is a sample of the "Welcome Letter" that my customers get.

I offer to do one makeup lesson per month per student if they can't make their normal lesson time. If they are a "no show" they forfeit that lesson. I have that time reserved for them. If I had known they were going to be gone I could have scheduled something else for that time slot. You can be a little more flexible if you only have a few students, but you will find as you get busier there will be less time for makeup lessons.

Keeping Track of Student Info
I use an Excel spreadsheet workbook to keep track of my lesson schedule. One page has my weekly schedule. At a glance I can see what time students are scheduled for the week. That same page has a list of contact info for each student. I typically have at least one change in the schedule each week. I copy and paste the permanent schedule and make notes as to which students will be gone and when makeup lessons will be.

Within the workbook each student has their own page. This page lists all the days they are scheduled for weekly lessons. I mark what day they paid and the amount. Each week I put an "x" if they are there for their lesson. I mark "gone" or "no show" if they are absent. No show means they were absent and did not notify me they would not be there.

I have another page in the workbook that gives an overview of payment records. It has each student's name in the left column. The months of the year are the top row. When a student pays for lessons, the amount gets put in the column for that month. This way at a glance I can see which students have paid and which ones have not. The bottom row is set up to total all the monthly payments. The last column totals what each student has paid for the year, with a grand total for the year at the bottom of that column. If you know a little about Excel, this is an easy workbook to create.

Summary
Besides a profitable business venture, teaching people to play music is very rewarding. I enjoy helping people learn to play an instrument. Now that you're armed with all this information, get out there and start making money in the guitar biz!

The next page is a sample of my "Welcome Letter" to new students.

Welcome!

Thank you for choosing me to give you, or your son or daughter guitar lessons. I have been playing the guitar and bass for over 30 years and giving lessons throughout those years. The guitar and music in general, has been a great source of enjoyment for me. My goal is to help my students learn the guitar so they can enjoy the many benefits of playing an instrument.

I believe in starting out with the basics, such as reading music and learning where the notes and chords are on the guitar. From there we can go to more advanced things, like learning specific songs, or improvisation.

Each lesson you will be given a section to practice. I recommend students practice at least a half hour a day. As with anything, the more you do it, the easier it becomes. If you don't practice, it is hard to advance to the next level. I have found some good material that keeps it interesting and fun.

Payment and Attendance Policies

Lessons are $_____ per half hour lesson. Payment is due at the beginning of each month. Example: If your lessons are on Monday, and there are 4 Mondays in that month, $_____ is due on the first Monday of the month. The expectation is that you pay for all the lessons in a month. Make-up lessons are available if you are unable to make your time slot. (see below). A $5.00 late fee will be charged if payment is not made the first week of the month. Please be on time for your lesson, so that there are not delays for other students.

Make-up lesson policies: If you are unable to make your scheduled time, I will work with you to schedule a makeup lesson within the same month. *If you are not able to make it to your lesson please call me as much in advance as possible. If* *you are a "no show" without calling, you pay for that lesson, and will not make it up.* Likewise, there may also be occasions where I am not able to give a lesson at the scheduled time. In those instances I will contact you as far in advance as possible and attempt to reschedule for that week. Only one makeup lesson per month per student will be allowed with a maximum of 6 makeup lessons per year. If your current lesson time needs to be changed to avoid makeup lessons, let me know. I am always glad to work with you.

Student Info

Name _____

Parent's name (if applicable) _____

Phone _____

Signature _____

E-Mail: _____

Thank you again for choosing me as your guitar instructor. Please see my website for repair and other services I offer. I also stock guitar strings and accessories, so if a string gets broken or it's time for new ones (I recommend every 6 months), let me know.

Thank you,
Alan Morrison
LIKE AM Guitar Works on Facebook
FOLLOW @AMGuitarWorks on Twitter
Website: www.amguitarworks.com
E-Mail: amguitars@mchsi.com

Chapter 3

Performing

I am assuming that if you are reading this book, you play guitar or another instrument. You may already be involved in performing either as a solo artist or as a member of a band. There are many opportunities to make money performing.

Very few people are fortunate enough to make their entire living playing music. However, it's a good way to make a little extra money. Besides, what's more fun than playing music in front of people?

If you're not currently in a band, the quickest way to start making money is to join an established band. Check local music stores, internet social media music groups, etc. If you can find an established band, you can start making money right away. Be prepared for an audition.

There are several factors that will determine your potential to make money playing music. These factors include:
- How much time and effort do you want to put into it?
- What are your music skills?
- What are your musical tastes?
- What are the opportunities in your area?
- What stage of life are you in?

The main thing I will do with this chapter is go through my experiences playing in bands. I have played in bands since high school and I am now over 50. Over the years, all the factors listed above have changed, but I still enjoy playing as much as I did in my high school years. When I see that bands I grew up listening to are still out there playing, it gives me confidence that I'll be able to continue playing music for people for several more years.

I joined my first band when I was in high school. I was 16 years old and the band was called Phantasy. I was referred to this band by my guitar teacher. We had many rehearsals and only a few gigs. My first paid gig was with this band on New Year's Eve 1980. It was a party for a hair styling school where our drummer's mother worked. I made $26.00 at this gig. Even though I made very little money with this band, I was honing my guitar skills and learning to play with other musicians. Gaining these skills would prepare me for future gigs.

During my college years I played in two bands. The first band was Ramblin' Fever. This was an established band that needed to replace their lead guitarist. We played country, 50's and 60's. We would do a set of 50's and 60's music with me dressed as Buddy Holly. Then we would put on cowboy hats and do a set of music from *Urban Cowboy* which was a popular movie at the time.

At the same time, a couple friends of mine said they wanted to start a band. One was an experienced drummer and the other was someone who wanted to learn to play bass. We started out as a three piece band called Puro. I gave the bass player some lessons and we learned some easy songs. If you're familiar with rock from the 70's, you know that if you knew a few chords and could figure out some riffs, there were plenty of songs that you could play.

25

Our first rehearsal space was a barn out in the country where we could crank things up and not bother anyone. Later we added a keyboard player who let us practice in his basement.

Many of our rehearsals turned into private party gigs. We started booking performances for high school dances, wedding receptions and firemen's dances. We rehearsed more than we gigged, but it was more preparation for the next level.

A couple of years after college, I was working as a technician/guitar teacher/retail salesperson at Ottmar Music Center, a music store in Atlantic, IA. One day a member of the band Bentwood walked into the store and asked if there were any new guitar players in town. He said he knew all the old ones and wasn't interested in them. I said I was new in town and would be interested in playing in a band.

Bentwood was based in Adair, a small western Iowa town. I auditioned and made the band. They were well established and played for lots of gigs in all the small towns around that area. We played weddings, firemen's dances, town celebrations, private parties, etc. We were playing three to four gigs a month at $100-$200 per person. It was a nice supplemental income to someone making $6.00 per hour working in a music store. It paid for my wife's wedding ring, a used car that we needed, and lots of groceries.

Even after I moved to the Des Moines area for a higher paying job, I continued to drive to western Iowa to play with this band. We spent lots of time playing, and very little time rehearsing.

We would get together once or twice a year to learn some new material.

In 1998, an opportunity for a promotion moved me to Davenport, IA. I had been in Bentwood for 13 years – the same 4 guys. We had seen members get married, have children, and watched each other's kids grow up. It was like a family and the decision to move away was very difficult, but it was the right career move for me at the time. I have many fond memories of playing with that band and still keep in touch with the members and their families.

After moving to Davenport, I started looking for another band. It gets in your blood and it becomes a part of who you are.

I was filling in occasionally for a house band that played every Friday and Saturday night at a bar. A couple of the members of that band were a husband and wife that had become family friends. They asked me if I'd be interested in forming a band with them. The house band gig was getting very time consuming and they wanted to play less and make more money.

We formed a 3 piece band called "The Wedding Singers". The band was myself on guitar, Dave on keyboards, and his wife, Carrie, sang. We used MIDI tracks for drums and bass and other instrumentation. This was a new experience for me. We made it work and splitting up band money between three people was pretty nice.

I received a phone call one day in 2004 from the music director of a community theatre production who asked me if I would play guitar for a musical production of *Das Barbeque*. I was referred to him because I was a guitar player who could read music, which is sometimes hard to find. This is an example of another opportunity to earn money performing.

While rehearsing and performing for the musical, I got to know the drummer, who was also my son's 7th grade band director at the time. After the musical was over he told me he was interested in starting a rock band with a full horn section. We would play classic rock tunes. I thought this sounded like fun. He showed up at my doorstep one day with a three ring binder full of charts and said, "Rehearsal is on Sunday".

The name of the band is Identity Crisis, and I am still in the band. The band fits a niche because we have 12 people on stage – male and female singers, bass, drums, keyboards, two guitarists, two trumpets, sax, flute, trombone and violin. There are few bands that can pull off a lot of the material that we can do because of our instrumentation. Most of the members are either band directors or veteran rockers like me who have been playing since our high school days. We play lots of weddings, corporate events, and larger clubs and venues.

I attribute the band's success to having dedicated talented players, and we play music that our audience grew up listening to. Music can bring back memories from our younger days. If you play what people enjoy, you will draw a crowd. If you draw a crowd, the establishment you are working for makes money. If they make money, you get invited back.

Working as a Solo Artist or Accompanist
This part of the chapter will be the shortest, because it is not my specialty. I have, however, made money playing as an

accompanist for singers, string players, and flautists at weddings. These gigs usually pay pretty well and you may only have to learn a couple of songs. I usually charge $100 if all I have to do is show up at the wedding and play. I charge an extra $50 if I have to be at the rehearsal. I also make sure that printed music is provided or reimbursed. Team up with singers or other instrumentalists. If you're comfortable with this type of gig, make up a business card and give wedding planners your contact information.

Performing as a Full Time Touring Musician
During the course of writing this book, I was privileged to meet Derek Williams, a professional touring guitarist. He has been a sideman for Jake Owen, Florida Georgia Line, LeAnn Rimes, Billy Gibbons, and many other acts. He was in town for a Jake Owen concert and met with a group from QC Rock Academy, a local lesson studio.

He had lots of good advice and gave me permission to quote him for this project. It was mainly a Q&A session. Here are some of the questions and answers.

How old were you when you realized that you wanted to be a professional musician?
Derek: I grew up in Nashville, and I started playing guitar when I was 10. My mother was a bass player in a rock and roll band and my great grandfather was the house piano player at the Grand Ole Opry, so I was held to a standard. I was into Thrash Punk and Heavy Metal, but my first paid gig was with a country act opening up for Dolly Parton at the Grand Ole Opry. It was cool to think I was on the same stage where Johnny Cash and Kris Kristofferson performed.

In high school, I took the aptitude test that helped determine what profession I was best suited for. I only answered yes to three questions and they all had to do with music. The test showed that I should be a professional musician. I got in trouble with the principal and was told "you can't do that." I was like, "Why not? Someone has to do it".

What steps did you take to achieve your goal?
Derek: I studied music in college, specifically classical guitar. I played in metal bands. I played in Christian rock bands as well. It was through the Christian rock scene that I made connections in the country music industry. Even though I love metal, country music is where the money is. I had to decide if I wanted to play metal shows for $300 split between 5 guys or do I want to make $500 a show for myself playing country?

What advice would you give someone who wants to be a professional touring musician?
Derek: Learn the rules and break them. Don't be afraid to make mistakes. Music is not about perfection. When I was learning classical guitar, I pressured myself and thought everything had to be perfect. My professor told me that the imperfections in music are what make it art. I like to make my first mistake early on in the show, so I get it out of the way. Then the pressure is off and I can relax and enjoy myself. *(Derek was wearing a shirt that read "Perfect Is Boring" when we met for this session).*

You don't have to be a virtuoso to play music for a living. There are some very technical players out there, but they aren't necessarily the ones filling arenas with thousands of screaming fans. I spend most of the show playing power chords and some lead licks. It's attainable for anyone. Someone has to do it. Why not you?

It's important to be versatile. The more instruments you can play, the better off you'll be. There is lots of competition in this business.

Have stage presence. Get into the music. Practice in front of a mirror so you know what you look like. If you went to a concert and the musicians were just standing there looking at their shoes, you would be disappointed. You'd ask for your money back. Don't be shy about it.

It's also important when touring to stay in shape. I try to exercise every day. Eat a banana before the show. Potassium calms the nerves.

What is the most difficult part of what you do for a living?
Derek: No personal space. I wake up on a bus with 11 dudes. It's hard to get away and withdraw to get some peace.

What do you like most about your profession?
Derek: Performing. It's a natural high to get out in front of people. There's no other feeling like it. Once you do it, you always want to do it.

Derek has set up a webpage at www.thatsmygig.com. It is a website that has free information to help people who want to make music their career. You can even use the website to connect with Derek or a number of other music industry people for one on one consultation.

I would like to give a huge "thank you" to Derek for sharing his thoughts on performing as a professional touring musician.

Summary

Throughout my performing career, I have been lucky to have been part of established bands and also startup bands.

The one thing they all have in common was that I got involved with them through networking. You have to talk to people. You need to go to the places where musicians hang out. You need to practice your instrument and play well with others so you are ready for an audition when the opportunity arises. When preparation meets opportunity, great things happen.

As far as the money aspect of it, if I counted the hours spent rehearsing, traveling, setting up, performing, and tearing down, the hourly rate doesn't always come out to be the best. However, if you can make a few hundred dollars every month as a "weekend warrior", it can add up. Plus, it's fun to play music for people.

You can also look at it as another networking opportunity. I have signed up guitar students and found customers in need of my repair business at gigs as well. One of the guitars I play is the demo model for my Guitar Building 101 class. As you read this book, you will see how each activity generates synergy and directs revenue to other aspects of my business.

Remember our "Basic Business Strategy #1?
Basic Business Strategy #1
1. Create a product or offer a service – Performing is a service, entertainment is the product.

2. Find customers who are willing to pay for your product or service – Find venues to play or established bands in need of your service.
3. Keep the customers coming back and get them to refer others – Draw the crowds and you will be invited back to the venue.
4. Network to grow the business – Networking is HUGE. There is an entire chapter dedicated to it later in this book.

Chapter 4

Guitar Repair and Customizing

Are you mechanically inclined? Good at basic woodworking?
Know some basic electronics? Like tinkering with guitars?
Guitar repair and customizing is another great way to make
money in the guitar biz.

This chapter is not going to be focused on how to repair and
customize guitars, but how to make money at it. There are
several resources available that will help you learn guitar repair
and those will be discussed in this chapter as well. You may
already be skilled at repairing or customizing guitars, but not
sure how to break into the business. Maybe you are in the
business, but looking for tips to take your business to the next
level.

I first started my journey of guitar building and repairing while
in high school, building my own electric guitar. I highly
recommend if you are interested in repairing guitars, that you
build a guitar – not necessarily from scratch, but put together a
project guitar. There are guitar kits that are available for very
little money. By assembling a guitar, you learn how everything
works and how it fits together.

Before getting into the business full time, I was building guitar
kits for some of my students. They were unfinished, so I was
able to develop my painting and finishing skills. They also
required lots of setup to get them to play properly.

Besides learning finishing and assembly skills, you need to know how to wire and troubleshoot guitar electronics. You don't need a college degree in electronics to repair guitars, but a basic understanding of simple circuits is important and will help. Again, there are many resources available on this subject.

So how do you make money in the repair business? It goes back to our Basic Business Strategy.

Basic Business Strategy #1
1. Create a product or offer a service – Repair work or customizing is a service.
2. Find customers who are willing to pay for your product or service – Guitars are mechanical devices made of wood, plastic, metal and electronics. They are going to break. Also, many musicians like their instruments customized to fit their needs or achieve the sound or feel they are looking for.
3. Keep the customers coming back and get them to refer others – Do excellent work and you will get repeat business and referrals
4. Network to grow the business – Networking is HUGE in this business. There is an entire chapter dedicated to it later in this book.

Getting Started
Guitar repair requires more of an initial investment than the activities discussed in previous chapters. You have to spend money to make money, right?

You have to decide how far you want to go with this. Do you want to make a little extra money on the side doing basic repairs, or do you want to go full time and do major repairs?

If you still need to develop your skills, don't quit your day job...yet. I started out part time doing basic repairs out of my home, then went full time in a home-based business, then to commercial space, then to a larger commercial space.

Educate Yourself

There are several resources to get you started in guitar repair – some costing less than others. There are books, DVD's, online resources such as YouTube videos, internet guitar forums, all the way up to luthier schools.

Start with the lowest cost ways first, such as books and DVD's. I highly recommend the following books: *How To Make Your Electric Guitar Play Great* which includes a set of plastic radius gauges, which are useful tools. *Guitar Player Repair Guide* includes a guitar maintenance DVD. Both books are by Dan Erlewine, who is a highly respected luthier.

The next level of educating yourself that I recommend is through the Dan Erlewine Repair Series of DVD's. These cost around $50 each, but are well worth the money if you consider it an investment in educating yourself. These are available through Stewart MacDonald. Their website is www.stewmac.com.

For more advanced training, you may want to try to get an apprenticeship at a local shop. You can also attend classes on guitar repair and guitar building. I teach a guitar building class that covers assembling a solid body electric guitar. We cover assembly techniques, wiring the electronics, and final setup. It's a weekend class where people assemble guitars made from pre-cut, pre-finished parts. More details on this later in the book. You can go to www.amguitarworks.com to look at class schedules.

I attended a fretwork class at Chicago School of Guitar Making, aka Specimen Guitars. I had watched the fretwork DVD's, but felt I needed more hands-on training with an experienced luthier. This class involved doing a complete refret on your own guitar. If you're serious about guitar repair, fretwork is a must.

Customizing Guitars
Guitarists are always looking for ways to upgrade or customize guitars to meet their needs or find the ultimate tone. There are many electronic mods and aftermarket hardware that you need to become familiar with. You can make money selling and installing these on guitars for your customers. Subscribe to magazines and join online guitar forums to keep up with the latest trends.

What You Need to Know
If you are going to start a repair business here are the things you should know how to do.

You need to know how to properly set up a guitar. A setup is adjusting the guitar to play properly for the customer's needs. Most customers like a low action. Action is the distance from the strings to the frets. If the action is too low, you will get fret buzz or notes fretting out. If the action is too high, the instrument will be difficult to play.

The adjustments for a basic setup include adjusting neck relief via the truss rod adjustment, nut slot depth, bridge saddle or bridge height adjustment, setting intonation, pickup height, and balancing the tremolo if applicable. You should know how to balance a standard tremolo as well as locking systems, such as Floyd Rose, Ibanez Edge, and Kahler tremolos.

You should also know how to do fretwork. If you set up a guitar to the correct specs, but are still getting fret buzz or fretting out, that usually means you have high or uneven frets. You need to know how to remedy this. I also recommend that you learn to re-fret an instrument. The more you know how to do, the more competitive you'll be and the financial rewards will be greater.

Another skill I recommend is learning how to make a nut from scratch. That is taking a rectangular piece of bone or other material and cutting, shaping, sanding, slotting, polishing and installing a perfectly fit nut on a guitar.

You should know how to do electronic repairs and modifications. Know how to replace pickups, pots, jacks and other items. Understand how acoustic/electric guitar electronics work. Learn how to install an undersaddle pickup system in an acoustic guitar.

If you are going to be a full service repair shop, you need to know how to repair cracks in acoustic guitars, repair broken headstocks, and do finish repairs. You may want to learn how to do a complete refinish on a guitar.

Knowing how to do all these things will differentiate you from your competitors and bring you more business. Knowledge and skills are power.

You can get these skills by taking classes, building guitars, or performing these repairs on your own instruments. If you don't want to learn on your prized possessions, buy cheap used guitars and practice on those.

Tools

If you are going to start repairing guitars, you will need some specialized tools. For doing setups, you will need an accurate straightedge, radius gauges, rulers, an assortment of Allen wrenches, needle files, nut slotting files, feeler gauges, and basic hand tools such as wire cutters and needle nose pliers.

Fretwork requires lots of specialized tools. Fret pullers, leveling tools, fretting hammer and fret setter, crowning, beveling and fret end files. You can also get fret pressing tools. Once the tools are paid for, fretwork can be very profitable.

For electronics work you need a decent soldering iron. For guitar electronics, I highly recommend a variable temperature soldering station. The reason for this is different soldering situations have different ideal soldering temperatures. Guitar electronics involve soldering ground connections to the backs of volume and tone potentiometers (pots). This requires a little more heat than making regular connections. On guitars with tremolo tailpieces, the ground wire is usually soldered to the spring claw which requires higher temperatures as well. These higher temperatures may be too hot for standard connections.

I use a Weller WLC100 variable temperature soldering station. I paid around $50 for it and use it almost daily. It has worked well for years. All I've had to do is change tips a few times. The temperature control goes from 1-5. I set it on 3 for normal soldering, 4 for soldering to backs of pots, and 5 for soldering to tremolo spring claws.

When it comes to tools there are a couple ways to go depending on your budget. If you can afford it, spend a little more and get the good tools. If you're on a budget, you can go with lower priced items and get the good stuff as your business grows. I have learned that buying cheap tools rarely pays off. You pay for the cheap tools, then they don't work or break and you end up spending money for the higher quality tools anyway.

AM Guitar Works has some basic tools available for sale on our website. Stewart MacDonald is my go to place for tools that I am unable to get through my suppliers. They have been around for years and are very reputable. I've saved money by building some specialized tools myself.

Many guitar tools may seem expensive to the hobbyist. However, once you go into a full time repair business, you will quickly learn the meaning of the phrase "time is money". Many of these "expensive" tools pay for themselves as they allow you to do a better job and more efficiently.

Certain major repairs may require specialized tools to complete the job. When I started part time, if I took on a job that would require purchasing specialized tools, I would make sure the estimate was at least enough to cover my cost of the tools. Sometimes I broke even on those repair jobs, but I had the right tools to do similar repairs in the future. After several years in the business I've built up quite a collection of items that make my shop more efficient and also help me turn out higher quality work.

Work Area

You will need a good well lit work area, a good solid workbench, and storage for tools and parts. I highly recommend being organized when it comes to this.

Again, time is money. If you are spending too much time looking for tools or parts that have been misplaced, you are losing money.

My main work area has two 20" x 5' workbenches back to back that I purchased from Harbor Freight. If you watch for sales, you can get these benches for around $130 each. I built a couple of tool holders that are attached to the workbench that has the most commonly used tools handy. Each bench has four drawers and a storage shelf. There are also woodworking vises on each bench. My setup bench has my setup tools in the drawers. Another bench is equipped for fretwork with a luthier vise and fretting tools in the drawers. I may end up with a lot of tools out for a repair job, but once that job is completed, everything goes back to its designated place so I know where to find it the next time I need it.

I also have a separate table that is the correct height for sitting while doing detail or electronic work. There is also a power tool workbench in my shop with a drill press, belt sander, scroll saw, sanding block, etc. This bench is in a separate area because it is usually where I generate wood and bone dust. I always look for

41

built in storage drawers and shelves when purchasing a bench. You can never have enough storage or be too organized.

Parts

You will need good resources for parts. If you are going into business you will want to get dealerships with guitar part suppliers so you can get discounted prices on parts.

Each supplier has unique requirements for becoming a dealer. The main thing is that you are a legitimate business with a sales tax license. Most distributors require a minimum initial purchase to become a dealer. Some companies require you to have an actual store front rather than a home-based business.

For getting started, I highly recommend Allparts. They carry a full line of guitar parts and have great customer service. They have been my main part supplier and I order from them at least a couple times per month. As you expand your business, you will find other companies that you will want to do business with as well.

Just like your tools, you will want to keep your parts organized. Know what you have on hand and where they are located. My shop has lots of drawers, labeled and organized by part types.

You will also want to keep strings on hand. The larger quantity of strings you buy, the lower the price per set. I keep a few different brands on hand in the shop in the most common gauges.

Also keep individual strings of the lighter gauges on hand. Lighter gauge strings sometimes get broken during the repair process and you don't want to have to break up a complete set to get one string.

Marketing Your Repair Business

You've educated yourself, set up your workbench, and have some parts and strings on hand. How do you go about generating cash?

You need to market yourself and your business. In a later chapter in this book, I will go into more detail on marketing, advertising strategies and dealing with competition. In this chapter I will discuss ideas specific to the repair business.

When you are a guitar repair person, you are selling your time, skills, knowledge and expertise. In many areas of the country, guitar repair is a niche business. Lots of music stores have repair people, but they may not do in depth repairs such as refrets, electronic mods, finish repairs, etc. If you can do those things, you become more valuable. I have people who bring guitars to me that are from other states because they don't have a reputable shop in their area equipped to do advanced repairs.

In order to make money you need to find customers and customers need to find you. You need to have a website with good SEO (Search Engine Optimization). There are several templates out there that you can use to set up a website. If you don't have a clue on setting up a website, hire someone to do it for you. The price will vary greatly. If you know someone good at web design and they happen to play guitar, you may be able to trade services. Bartering for services is an excellent business strategy.

I designed my first website using Microsoft Front Page. That website was not the greatest and you could probably tell it was "home grown" by an amateur. However, people found me on it and I stayed very busy. My web host provider took care of the SEO keywords. If you Googled "guitar repair Quad Cities" (or any of the four city names or surrounding area), references to AM Guitar Repair filled most of the first two pages. AM Guitar Repair was at the top of the list except for the paid listings. I don't pay for my Google listing, because I have so much coverage already.

You will also want to use social media marketing, such as Facebook, Instagram and Twitter. More details on this in a later chapter.

When I moved to a new location and AM Guitar Repair changed to AM Guitar Works, I needed a new website. My current website was designed by The Gunter Agency. They designed a WordPress website and trained me how to update the text and photos.

Besides having a website, you need to network, network, and network some more. Get some business cards printed. You can design your business cards on a computer and print them on your home printer. However, I highly recommend having your cards printed professionally if you are serious about this. Just like websites, some "home grown" business cards look like they were printed at home. Commercially printed cards make you look more professional and present a better image.

If you are a guitar player, I am going to assume that you have some friends or family members who also own guitars. If you are doing some of the other activities in this book, such as giving lessons or performing, you have some pools of potential customers. Make sure all your friends and family have business cards for themselves and to hand out to people they run across who may need your services.

Take your business cards to music stores, lesson studios, and other places where musicians hang out. I've generated business by going to hear bands and handing out business cards to band members during breaks.

Always have business cards with you wherever you go. I have a small business card holder and I don't leave home without it. Just like my wallet or cell phone, it's always with me. You can put business cards in your wallet, but with all the other items in your wallet it's easy to forget to restock it. I always know when my business card holder is empty.

When going to music stores, understand that they may have a repair person on staff. Find out how in-depth their repairs are. If you go beyond that, they may give you some business. If they don't have a repair person on staff, they may be interested in referring repairs to you or contracting with you to do repairs for them.

When I first got into the repair business, I went to a local lesson studio. The owner and I made a deal where they got a percentage of any of the work that I did. I was working part time out of my house, and they were located a couple blocks away. I would pick up and deliver there. At that time, I was hungry to get into the business and gave away a bigger percentage than I should have, but it did generate business for me and I was able to gain some new clients.

Shortly after that, I ended up being the repair center for a large guitar store. This came through networking and talking with the store manager on a regular basis. They were shipping items out of state to be repaired and were dealing with long turnaround times. I convinced the store manager their customers would be happier if the items were repaired locally with quicker turnaround time.

I was doing pickup and delivery there as well. Many times they just referred customers to me directly. They did not ask for a cut of the repair bill and I did not discount for them. They may have marked up my repairs to their customers, but I was getting my full price. Between all the work and new customers they were sending to me, along with the networking I was doing on my own, I was able to go full time in the guitar business within a year.

Eventually that store changed management and hired an in-house repair person. By that time, though, I had a big enough customer base that my business stayed steady and continued to grow. They also still refer people to me for advanced repairs and amplifier repairs.

The best advertising you will get is word of mouth, mainly referrals. Guitar players usually have multiple instruments. Guitar players also tend to hang out together. Some play in bands with each other. With every repair that comes across my bench, I keep in mind that this repair could generate multiple repairs. Those repairs may be other instruments from the same owner, or their friends' guitars. Make them happy and you will get repeat business and referrals.

Setting Your Rates

This is one of the most difficult parts of the business – deciding how much to charge. This issue is not limited to the guitar business. I have talked to many small business owners, and they mention this challenge as well. I cannot tell you what to charge, because it depends on how well you're established, your skill levels and experience, your geographic location, and your competition situation. What I can tell you are some of the answers given to me when I've asked for advice on this subject.

I price my repairs two different ways. Some services I offer are a flat rate. Setups are a flat rate depending on the type of guitar. Basic setups on an acoustic guitar or a hard-tail electric guitar are the least involved, so are my lowest priced setups. My setups include truss rod adjustment, bridge or saddle height adjustment, nut slot depth adjustment, tightening tuner hardware, oiling the fingerboard, re-stringing, intonation adjustment, cleaning and polishing. I charge extra for guitars with tremolo bridges, and even more for guitars with locking nuts and tremolos. There are additional fees if the setup requires removal of the neck for shimming or truss rod adjustment. I also charge extra if the setup requires removal and shimming or replacing the nut. Any fretwork required is an additional charge as well.

Other repairs are done based on an hourly rate. When quoting these, I try to estimate the amount of time it's going to take for each step of the repair process and take that times the hourly rate.

When estimating, keep this in mind. The job will usually take longer than you think it will. Allow time for the unexpected.

I've talked to other small business owners and experts about setting rates. Here are some of the answers I've gotten:

- One answer was, "A little bit less than your competition".
- Another answer was "A little more than your competition. If you are priced too low, people will think you don't do a good job." I like this answer better.
- "5 to 10 percent above what you're charging now." This answer was given to me by a professional consultant at a business conference. He gave me this answer without even knowing what my rates were. He did this based on his prior experience with small business owners who were priced too low.
- Something to take into consideration is that more and more people are paying with debit or credit cards. Depending on the service you use to accept those cards, keep in mind that the service may get around 3% of the transaction. People will tend to spend more if they can use plastic, but it costs you, the business owner to accept those types of payments. I highly recommend you have the ability to accept credit and debit cards. More info on this in a later chapter.
- Another answer given by a professional business consultant – "You're priced too low if 10% of your customers don't complain about your pricing." This is a tough one, but makes sense. How often do we as consumers take our car in to a mechanic and are thrilled with the estimate we get? We need the car to work, so

we pay the price and move on. I have a car shop that I trust and am loyal to. Repairs usually seem expensive, but they are lower priced than taking the car to a dealer. I am willing to pay what they charge because I trust them, they are courteous, professional, and they have always done quality work. Any issues after the repair are quickly resolved.

- Listen to your customers. This is somewhat related to the above bullet point. I cannot tell you how many times I have given an estimate or a repair bill to a customer and heard quotes like this: "That's VERY reasonable." "I thought it would be much more than that." "That's way less than what I was quoted somewhere else." That's when you hang up the phone and kick yourself for quoting too low. You may have quoted a little on the low side because you wanted the work and were afraid if you were too high, the estimate would be refused. If you are getting responses like this, it's time to raise your rates. People expect to pay for quality work. Make sure you do quality work and that your rates reflect that accordingly.

- Supply and demand: If you have built up a reputation and have lots of work coming in and are finding it hard to keep up, you should be able to adjust your rates as well. There is a demand for your service. If you have little or no competition, you can charge accordingly. If your overwhelmed with workload, you have no excuse if you're struggling to make ends meet.

- Give yourself a raise. I raise my rates a little each year. I am self-employed, so I don't get an annual review and pay increase like I did when working in the corporate world.

- Remember why you are in business – to make money. While you are providing a service that is in demand and is personally satisfying, in order to stay in business and meet your financial needs, you have to make money. It costs money to run a business and you have to pay yourself as well. More on this in a later chapter.

What About the Customer Who Says Your Price Too High?
My labor rates have always been in line with other shops in my area. Lower than some and higher than others.

I recently quoted a price via e-mail to cut a custom nut from scratch and ship it to a customer. I gave my quote and they replied, "Why so much?"

I explained that my labor rates cover my time, experience and knowledge. I have to cover the cost of specialized tools that it takes to do my work. The rates also have to cover rent of my shop, utilities, insurance, phone, internet, payroll, etc., and I have to pay myself a little bit as well because this is how I make my living. I have many of the same costs at home as well.

So what do you do when you quote a price and the customer doesn't want to spend the money? Let's say for example a customer needs major work done with multiple issues and you quote $400. If the customer states that they don't want to spend that much money, ask them what they are willing to spend. If they say $250, let them know how much of the work can be done for that price. Maybe the job can be partially done, and the rest finished at a later date.

Business Ethics and Honesty
With all the above talk about money, it is appropriate to follow up with a discussion about business ethics and honesty. If you

try to cheat your customers or use unethical business practices, people will find out about it. People don't like to be ripped off, deceived or misled. Word travels quickly with all the social media technology that is available these days. If you do these types of things in order to make a fast buck, it will catch up to you. You will lose business, and ultimately go out of business.

Being honest and ethical will allow you to have a clear conscience and you will be more successful in the long run. Always think long term.

Continuing Education

I love the repair and customizing business because there is such a wide variety of skills and knowledge involved. There are sometimes challenging situations for which you need to figure out creative solutions. Stay up to date on mods and what is popular for upgrades. Learn as much as you can about various types of repair. To gain experience, buy cheap guitars that need repair work and practice on those. Customize your own guitars with mods so you can demo them for customers.

A great resource is internet forums. Reranch is one of the forums I have learned the most on. Reranch is also a supplier of guitar lacquers and finishing materials. It's made up of a great group of knowledgeable people with years of experience in guitar work.

Subscribe to magazines related to your business. Know the new products that are coming out.

Read books regarding running a business or staying motivated.

Finally, to see what goes on at AM Guitar Works, you can follow our Facebook page. I often post "Shop Shots", pictures of repairs in progress, or sometimes the whole process from beginning to end.

One of my customers has a tag line at the end of his e-mail: "Learn something new every day." Good advice.

Chapter 5

Amplifier Repair and Customizing

Amplifier repair is another way to make money in the guitar biz, provided you have the knowledge and the tools. A good working knowledge of electronics is necessary. If you are a young person considering career choices, an electronics degree will come in handy for guitar and amplifier repair.

If you know electronics, this chapter will make sense. If you don't, the terminology may be unfamiliar. Keep reading though. It may be a challenge that you want to tackle at some point.

When I first started my guitar repair business, I told myself I wasn't going to offer amplifier repair, even though I had knowledge and experience. Amplifiers can be big, heavy, dirty and dangerous. The circuitry is more complex than guitars and troubleshooting can be challenging at times.

I soon changed my mind, however. I had been talking to a large music shop about taking on guitar repair work for them. They already had a plan for repairs, but it wasn't fitting their customers' needs as far as turnaround time.

One day they called me and asked if I worked on amplifiers. I wasn't going to tell them "no". I have an electronics degree and experience working on amps from my days at the music store in Atlantic.

The amplifier had been shipped to them with the tubes removed and they didn't know where to properly install them. I picked it up and brought it back the next day with an invoice. They wrote me a check on the spot.

On my way home I got a call from their regional manager who asked if I would be their local repair station. Of course I said "Yes!" This turned out to be a connection that would launch my business to the next level.

Repairing amplifiers has now become a large part of my business. There is not a lot of competition in this area for servicing amplifiers, so we get business from miles around.

Attention: Danger!
If you're going to work on amplifiers, you need to know electronics. You need to understand the dangers and safety precautions in order to be safe. There are lethal voltages lurking in amplifiers even when they are unplugged. The electrolytic filter capacitors can retain high voltages that will shock you if you touch them or anything connected to them. They need to be discharged before servicing an amplifier. Consider yourself warned.

What You Need To Know
Guitar amplifiers are basic compared to other electronic devices. Vintage tube amps are especially simple with no onboard digital effects. They consist of a power supply, preamp gain stages with volume and tone controls, and an output stage.

Basic solid state amplifiers are the same thing only with transistors or integrated circuits instead of tubes.

Both tube and solid state amplifiers may have a spring reverb tank and/or a tremolo circuit.

Tube technology was still being taught when I went to electronics school in the early 80's. If you're going to repair amplifiers, you need to study up on tube technology. There are several books and other resources on this subject listed in the "Resources" chapter at the end of this book.

I would estimate that at least 75% of the amplifiers I service are tube amps. They sound great, but tube technology is not as reliable as solid state. The high voltages and heat required to make a tube amp work take their toll on electronic components. With vintage amps, you are adding aged components into the equation with the high voltages and heat.

Tools Needed
In order to service amplifiers, you are going to need some specialized tools. Here is what I recommend at minimum:
- Tube tester – Look for these for sale online
- Volt ohm meter with built-in capacitance meter
- Variable temperature soldering iron
- Desoldering bulb, desoldering iron, solder wick.
- Audio generator (I built a simple audio generator from a kit purchased online for around $30)
- Signal trace probe (another gadget I made for under $10)
- Test speaker cabinet
- Tube Bias Checker (kits are available online)

- A ¼" wooden dowel or chopstick. I use these to look for bad solder joints. Poking around with this simple tool has helped troubleshoot a lot of intermittent problems.
- Oscilloscope – These come in handy sometimes, but I rarely use mine. It's not absolutely necessary. I use my audio generator and signal trace probe for tracking signals more often than the scope.

You will also want to keep an inventory of the most commonly used tubes on hand. The tube tester doesn't always tell the whole story. A tube may test "good", but it might have intermittent issues. Having known good tubes in stock to substitute will help you troubleshoot.

I keep a good supply of 12AX7, 12AT7, 12AU7, 6L6, 6V6, EL84, and 5Y3 tubes in stock. These are the most common tubes you will be replacing. Power tubes should be replaced in matched pairs, quads, or sextets, depending on the amplifier.

You will also need to know how to bias power tubes. This process is different for various amplifiers. Service manuals, schematics, and internet searches will help you find out how to bias most amplifiers.

Amplifier Maintenance
Amplifiers need maintenance from time to time. We offer "Tube Amp Tuneups" at our shop. A Tube Amp Tuneup includes:

- Check all tubes and replace as necessary
- Clean and re-tension tube sockets
- Adjust power tube bias
- Clean input and output jacks and replace as needed

- Clean and check potentiometers (controls) and replace as needed
- Check fuse size and replace if out of spec (safety issue)
- Check power supply filter capacitors and replace as necessary
- Check coupling capacitors
- Check resistors and replace if out of tolerance (mainly on vintage amps)
- Check reverb unit and repair if necessary
- Check speaker connections
- Clean inside of chassis
- Replace AC power cord with a 3 prong cord if the amplifier has a 2 prong or frayed power cord. (Safety issue)
- Check operation of amplifier

The last step is important. Once you've serviced an amplifier, it needs to run for a few hours to see if it has any hidden, intermittent issues. At minimum, plug a guitar in and let the amplifier idle for a few hours, occasionally strumming the guitar to make sure everything is still working properly.

As an even better test, I use my customer's amplifier for at least one session of lessons before declaring the amplifier ready to go. This gives the amp four to five hours of playing time. This has allowed me to catch hidden issues before giving the amplifier back to the customer.

We use this as a selling point of our amplifier repair service. Where else are you going to take an amplifier and have a technician play on it for five hours?

Typical Repairs

Many of the amplifier repairs I do are simple fixes if you have knowledge of electronics. Here is a list of some of the common problems you will see:

- Input jacks need replacement. Jacks wear out over time or get broken. On newer amps, they are usually a plastic housing and soldered onto the circuit board.
- Scratchy or intermittent controls. Spraying contact cleaner usually clears this up. Sometimes replacement is required to resolve the problem.
- Tubes need replacement. The tube tester and the wooden dowel come in handy for finding faulty tubes. Tapping them with a dowel can help spot microphonic tubes, or sometimes trigger that strange intermittent noise your customer told you about.
- Blown fuses. Amplifiers usually have a fuse that's accessible to the user. Some amplifiers also have internal fuses not accessible by the user. When replacing a fuse it's always good to check to see why it blew. Fuses blow for a reason. It may have just been a temporary power surge, though. Always use the correct value when replacing fuses.
- Blown speakers – Use your test speaker cabinet to check this.
- Filter capacitors need replacement – Excess hum in an amplifier is caused by electrolytic filter capacitors going bad. In vintage amps you can tell by looking at the seal on the caps. It will have blisters or you will see the electrolyte chemical leaking out.
- Reverb not working – Inside a reverb tank are small wires connecting the RCA style jacks to the tiny

transformers which connect to the springs. It's common for these wires to break and re-soldering them fixes the problem. Sometimes the transformers go bad. If that's the case, it's most cost effective to replace the tank. Most tanks have a code stamp or label that tells you which tank you need. Sometimes the RCA cables going from the amp to the reverb tank need replacement.

- Bad solder joints. Many intermittent problems can be traced to bad solder joints. The amp may work fine at first, but as components heat up they form an air bubble between the component lead and the solder. Bad solder joints may also be found on jacks as they get strained from plugging and unplugging cables. A wooden dowel helps you find these problems. If you poke around enough you can duplicate the problem and find the general area where the solder joint is bad. Try high heat components first, like power resistors. They can get hot and melt their own solder joints.

- Installing a 3 prong AC power cord. Many vintage amplifiers were made with 2 prong AC cords. This is a safety issue and can cause the user to get shocked since the amplifier is not properly grounded. If an amplifier comes in to my shop for repair with a 2 prong cord, I always recommend replacing it with a 3 prong cord.

Troubleshooting Low or No Signal Issues
Some repairs require obtaining a schematic diagram and tracing the signal to see where it gets weak or disappears. I use a signal generator that I built from a kit purchased online. It has a ¼" jack so I just run a guitar cable from the generator to the input of the amplifier. It generates a single audio frequency and has an amplitude (volume) control.

I use this in combination with a probe connected to a small inexpensive amplifier. You can make one by modifying an automotive logic probe. It has a pointed tip with an insulated handle. Use a shielded cable with a ¼' plug on one end.

- Connect the "hot" wire of the shielded cable to the tip of the probe. Connect the shield of the cable to a wire with an alligator clip on the end.
- Plug the signal generator into the input of the faulty amplifier and turn it on.
- Clip the alligator clip of your probe to a chassis ground on the amplifier you are troubleshooting. Plug the probe into a known good test amplifier.
- You now have signal going into the amplifier. Look at the schematic and follow the signal path. You can touch the probe to locations where the signal should be. Be careful that you only put the probe where there is supposed to be signal, not voltage!
- Once you find where you lose the signal or it gets weak, you are in the right area and can test the components in that part of the circuit.
- Once you find the bad component, check other parts in the same circuit that may have caused the problem. There can be a "domino" effect when electronic parts go bad.

Tech Tip: If the problem appears to be a faulty integrated circuit, install an IC socket prior to replacing. This will allow you to quickly remove the new IC if that wasn't the problem. If it was the problem, it will save you a lot of time if it goes bad again.

Parts Sources
There are several parts resources for amplifiers. My main suppliers for tube amplifier parts are CE Distribution and Mojo Musical Supply. Both carry tubes, capacitors, reverb tanks,

speakers and other parts for amplifiers. They also offer amplifier and pedal kits.

Mouser is a large electronics parts supplier. They carry resistors, capacitors, transistors, integrated circuits, diodes, and much more. Their catalog is the size of a phone book and their website is very detailed and provides all kinds of specs for each component.

An internet search will help you find parts not supplied by those listed above.

Summary
Many of strategies mentioned in the previous chapter on guitar repair apply to servicing amplifiers as well. You need a good working knowledge of electronics and safety procedures if you are going to be an amp tech. It is rewarding when an amplifier comes in for repair and you are able to bring it back to life. If you are up for the challenge, this is another way to make money in the guitar biz!

Chapter 6
Online Sales

There are lots of opportunities to make money in the guitar biz with online sales. eBay is probably the easiest and most common way to sell online. You can also set up other online stores as well. Be aware that there are lots of people selling guitar related items online so there is lots of competition. The key is to find a niche.

Here's how I got started selling online. When I started my repair business, many of the repairs that came in at first were electronic repairs. The parts that needed replaced were output jacks and volume and tone control pots. These are low priced items that are common to many makes and models of guitars. To order just a few small items the shipping charges are almost as much as the parts. I stocked up on these parts so I would have them on hand. Of course, soon after stocking up, these types of repairs slowed down.

I had inventory sitting around that I had paid for, and needed to turn into cash. I thought about selling the parts on eBay, but selling individual parts for only a few dollars each would not be worth the time to pack and ship. I came up with an idea on one of my morning walks. Why not bundle the components to make wiring kits for popular guitar and bass models?

This was my first experience with eBay. After researching what was available for wiring kits, I noticed a niche. There were some low priced kits with cheap components, and some high priced "boutique" wiring kits. "Boutique" usually means overpriced. I put together affordable kits with high quality components. With about 10 different items in different combinations, I had a dozen wiring kits listed and they slowly started selling. At first I was excited if one wiring kit sold per week. Then it was a few per week. Then it started averaging one per day. Pretty soon I was getting orders for multiple wiring kits almost every day. This kept growing and I expanded the types of wiring kits that I carried. They are still my top selling item, but sales have slowed down a little as there are now some other sellers offering kits similar to mine.

You always have to be actively looking for niches. As soon as you find a good one, others may see it and follow suit. They may try to undercut your pricing. Competition is part of being in business. I have held firm on my pricing. The ones who try to price too low eventually figure out it's not worth their time or it doesn't cover their expenses after fees are paid. Then they either raise their prices or go away.

Some of the other things I sell are items where I needed one part, but could only order in larger quantities. I had a customer bring me a mandolin for repair that had a broken nut. I had to order a package of 10 to get the one I needed. I listed the remaining nine on Ebay and they sold fairly quickly and at a decent profit margin. At that point I ordered another package of 10 just to sell online. Then I started ordering other small items in quantity and selling them as well. It's low risk and while you won't get rich selling these items, it is a good way to turn excess inventory into cash.

Also, if you're in the repair business, it's nice to always have these items on hand. Having a $3 part on hand may help you generate $65 quickly because you don't have to order a package of 10, pay shipping, and wait a week for it to arrive.

You have to make sure you have a good markup when selling smaller items and charge enough for shipping to make it worth your while. You also need a mix of higher priced items so that hopefully you are not spending precious time shipping out a few low priced items. You have to find the balance that works for you.

A short time after going full time in the repair business, my customers were asking what pickups I recommended. My existing part suppliers did offer pickups, but people weren't familiar with those brands. They were asking for more popular name-brand pickups. Then they would go to other stores, buy the pickups and pay me to install them.

At that point, I contacted a Seymour Duncan distributor. They require a minimum first order to become a dealer. I posted on a guitar forum that I was picking up a Seymour Duncan dealership and pre-sold half of the 24 pickups I needed for my initial order. These high quality American made pickups have sold very well for me.

As my repair business grew, I kept adding dealerships as situations arose. If you are just starting a small business, you want to go gradually. AM Guitar Works at the time of this writing is a dealer for the following companies: Allparts, Bill Lawrence USA, Cort Guitars, DiMarzio, Fishman, Gator Cases, Graph Tech, Harris-Teller, Hipshot Products, Jay Turser Guitars,

Jet City Amplification, Lava Cables, Mighty Mite Parts, Q Parts, Saga, Seymour Duncan, Sperzel, and Washburn Guitars. Some of these companies will work with home-based businesses. Others require you to have an actual retail store front.

Selling on eBay
eBay is the easiest way to get started selling online. There are entire books devoted to marketing and e-commerce so I am not going to go into a lot of detail. I will share the following tips based on my experiences and some good general advice.

If you don't have an eBay account, signing up is fairly straightforward.

You also need to have a Paypal account. Paypal is like an online bank account. The buyer's money goes into your account, minus the fee that Paypal collects. You can use the money in your Paypal account to purchase items online or transfer money to your bank account. Paypal also offers a prepaid debit card. You can use the card to purchase items as long as you don't exceed the amount in your account.

eBay Listing Types
There are a few different ways of selling on eBay. You can list items with a fixed price or you can have auction style listings where people bid on items. The highest bidder at the close of the auction wins the item. Auctions are good for one of a kind or used items.

Fixed Price Listings
Most of the selling I have done is fixed price where I have multiples of each item listed for sale. It costs the same to list

multiples of an item as it does to list one of those items. If you have 10 widgets to sell, you pay for the listing and it shows 10 are available. As people buy the widgets, the available number goes down accordingly. I have several items that I list for 30 days at a time. When the listing time ends, I check inventory and relist. These items are continuously restocked so I am never without inventory.

For items that you want to sell at a fixed price, but are not planning to immediately restock when you run out, there is a "Good 'Til Cancelled" option in the listing time choices. This means the item will be automatically relisted every 30 days until the available quantity is depleted.

Best Offer Option
Best Offer is an option that can go along with a fixed price item which makes the price of the item negotiable. This allows the potential buyer to click a "Make Offer" button and submit a dollar amount less than the fixed price. As a seller, you can accept their offer, make a counter-offer, or disregard their offer. I recommend making a counter-offer if you are not willing to accept the buyer's first offer.

As a seller if you chose the Best Offer option you should have an amount in mind that you are willing to take for the item. For example you are selling a guitar neck with a fixed price listing of $150 or best offer. Let's say you are willing to sell it for $140. If someone offers you $130, you can counter-offer $140.

Auction Listings
Auction type listings are good for selling used items or one of a kind items. Maybe you've got an item that has been a fixed

price item that has not sold in quite some time. You can auction it and at least get some money for it.

How an auction works is you list an item and people can bid on it. A typical auction listing is seven days. At the end of the listing time the highest bidder wins the item. When you list the item you set the initial price. I recommend setting a low initial price to attract and generate interest of potential buyers. People love getting a bargain. They also love winning. If you set the price low people will bid on it. Once some people get their mind set on winning an item, they will keep bidding until they win.

When doing an auction type listing, the end time of the auction is important. I usually try to have my auctions end on Sunday evenings. Most people are home winding down from the weekend and possibly shopping online. The more people you have bidding on your item at the last minute, the higher the bidding can go.

Reserve Price Option
If you have a minimum amount that you are willing to accept for an auction item, you have the option of setting a reserve price. Let's say you're auctioning a used guitar and you want to make sure that you get at least $200 for it. You can start the initial price at $99 and set a reserve price at $200. Bidders will not see the reserve price. If someone bids $150, they will get a "Reserve Not Met" message that tells them they will not win that item with their bid, but now the price is $150 because that is the highest bid. If the bidding does not reach the reserve price, the item will not be sold. Once the bidding reaches the reserve amount, the item is for sure going to be sold. It's just a matter of who has the highest bid at the end of the auction.

"Buy It Now" Option

The Buy It Now option can be added to an auction item. This is a fixed price that someone can pay for the item and override the bidding process. In our above example, we could add a Buy It Now price of $300. What that means is even if the bidding has started, the first person to click on Buy It Now button has made the purchase in the amount of $300 and the auction is over.

Item Title

You want people to be able to find your listings so make sure you use proper keywords in your listing titles. Think of what people might type in when they are searching for what you have to sell. You can make your listing stand out a bit by putting part of the title in all caps. Ebay allows you several characters to put in the title line so you can add a little more of a description.

For an additional fee, there is an option to add a subtitle line to give a few more details or offer a "bonus item" with purchase. For example your item title might be "SEYMOUR DUNCAN P-RAILS NECK PICKUP BLACK". A subtitle line might be "FREE MINI TOGGLE SWITCH INCLUDED".

Photos

Make sure to take quality photos of your items. Consistent backgrounds will also help people recognize the items as your product. Most of our smaller items, such as wiring kits, have their photos taken with a blue background. It's as simple as using a piece of colored paper. This is an easy way to start branding your company.

You can attach multiple photos to your listing. For example we sell guitar tools. We usually have the main picture be of the tool itself. We add pictures of the tools being used in "real life" situations. I believe this has increased our sales of those tools. You can have up to 12 pictures at no extra charge as of the time of this writing.

Descriptions

The description should be as complete as possible. Include brand names, dimensions (if applicable), color, etc. If the item has multiple uses, list them. Use bullet points for features. Think about what types of questions you might have if you were considering buying the item. The description area is also a good place to put more information about your business. Tell people what types of items you sell, brand names you carry, a link to your Facebook page, Twitter account or other social media.

Pricing

If you are selling a product you make yourself, you need to price it so that it is profitable. You will want to keep in mind that when you sell something on eBay, there are listing fees. eBay gets a fee when the item is sold, and Paypal collects a fee when the customer pays you. If you charge too low a price for your item, it will not be profitable. In order to survive, a business has to make money. If you are selling at a thin margin or losing money and time that could be spent on more profitable activities, your business won't last long.

If you are selling something that you are buying from a distributor and re-selling, there are probably some guidelines set by your supplier. MSRP (Manufacturer's Suggested Retail Price) is a guideline that can be used. If you contact a manufacturer to become a dealer, don't get too excited when you look at dealer cost and MSRP. It will look like you will make a lot of money selling that product. Look online and see what the item is actually selling for. Chances are it is selling lower, sometimes much lower, than MSRP. Consumers these days are not used to paying retail on larger items.

MAP Pricing

Many companies have a "Minimum Advertised Price" or MAP pricing for their products. This means that you cannot advertise the item for less than the MAP price. Companies do this for a couple of reasons. One reason is that people relate quality with price. Many companies don't want their products to be sold too cheap because it may give the impression that they are lower quality.

The other thing MAP pricing does is levels the playing field between the small business and large companies. In other words a big box store might be able to order in larger quantities and get the item for a lower price than a small business, but they cannot advertise it for less than MAP pricing. Items with MAP pricing are usually sold online for MAP pricing. People may offer free shipping or throw in a bonus item to be competitive.

Some people try to beat the MAP pricing game by advertising on eBay at the MAP pricing or "Best Offer". This may be acceptable practice by some suppliers, but other suppliers may not allow it.

Some sellers blatantly violate the pricing policies and advertise the item below MAP. When I have run across it, I turn them in to the distributor. Most distributors take this seriously and are very good at following up with these. They make them change their pricing or they can pull their dealership.

Personally, I prefer working with companies who use MAP pricing. I have worked with other companies who do not use it. I see their products selling on eBay for just a little above cost. After all the fees are taken out, I don't see how they make money. I have stopped ordering products I used to carry because of this. I told my rep I can't make money selling these online when the competitor is selling them at what has to be a loss or break even. I am sure I am not the only dealer who has experienced this with them.

Remember – the purpose of a business is to make money. If an item is not profitable, it doesn't make sense to spend time selling it.

Shipping Rates
When you are entering products on eBay, you will need to either choose free shipping, flat rate shipping, or calculate shipping. Keep in mind that besides the actual postage, there is the cost of the packaging. Envelopes, boxes, bubble wrap all have a cost associated with them.

We save packaging from items we receive and reuse as much as possible. I also have a couple places that supply us with small boxes and packing materials that they would otherwise throw away or send to the recycling bin. We save money every chance we get.

Something to keep in mind is that eBay takes a portion of the shipping that you charge as a fee. At one time they didn't take a cut of the shipping, but people were abusing the system. They were selling items at very low cost, but charging exorbitant shipping rates in order to make more profit.

Below is a list of the shipping options you have with Ebay.

Free Shipping

Free shipping is self-explanatory. I usually use free shipping on products that a lot of other people are selling with free shipping. This is usually the case with MAP pricing items, just because there are so many listed with free shipping and you have to be competitive. There are also things where people offer "Free Shipping" but the shipping is built into the price of the item.

Flat Rate Shipping

Flat rate shipping means everyone pays the same price for shipping regardless of their location. Some USPS, UPS, and Fedex rates are based on the distance an item has to be shipped. I use flat rate shipping on smaller items. I make sure that the shipping rate covers the cost of the postage and packaging and some of the fees.

Calculate Shipping

This option will calculate the shipping for the customer based on what the actual cost is to ship to them. You can add a percentage or a dollar amount to cover your packaging costs.

Managing Your Ebay Business

You've listed some items. Now what happens? Check your email often (at least daily) to see if anyone has questions or has made a purchase. Respond to questions quickly.

Shipping Items

Ship items quickly. We ship within one business day of receiving an order. You can pay for postage and print shipping labels through eBay or Paypal. If you have multiple items to ship, you can use the Paypal Multi-Order Shipping Tool.

Feedback

Feedback is an important part of eBay. It helps keep people accountable. Feedback allows buyers to rate their experience with a seller as Positive, Neutral, or Negative. Buyers and sellers both have a feedback percentage score with the best being 100%. Neutral scores do not count against the percentage, only negative. Besides selecting a rating, they can make comments. Some of your customers will be asked to rate you in certain categories on a 1 through 5 star rating in the following categories:

- Item as described
- Communication
- Shipping Time
- Shipping and handling charges

As a seller you want to make sure you keep your feedback rating high. How do you do this?

- Sell a quality product that is honestly represented.
- Ship items quickly at reasonable rates.
- Respond to questions quickly.
- Respond to customer complaints and resolve them quickly when they arise.

What If a Buyer Gives You Neutral or Negative Feedback?

eBay recommends that buyers contact the seller before leaving anything less than positive feedback. This gives the seller an opportunity to resolve the issue. Unfortunately, not everyone does this. If someone does contact you, resolve the issue quickly if possible.

For neutral or negative feedback situations, you as the seller, can fill out a "Feedback Change Request" that allows you to send a message to the buyer asking them to change the feedback and the reason(s) why. eBay also allows you to comment on the feedback that will be displayed on your feedback for all to see as well. This at least allows you to give your side of the story.

Leaving Feedback
Leaving feedback is an option on eBay. It is not required. I highly recommend that you leave feedback whether you are a buyer or a seller. According to my calculations we've only received feedback on 70% of the transactions we've done.

We always leave feedback when we purchase something on eBay. I leave feedback once a week. It's quicker to do several at a time.

eBay Stores
If you have several items you're selling, you can open up an eBay store with categories. You can find my store at stores.ebay.com/AM-Guitar-Repair

Other Online Sales Options
There are other options to selling online in addition to eBay. Most of the information covered so far in this chapter applies to any online store you may have. There's nothing wrong with having multiple places on the internet for people to buy your products. It's a matter of how much time you want to invest building and maintaining a store and shipping products. You can also consider hiring someone to do these tasks for you.

Besides my eBay store, I currently have online stores through Highwire and Reverb.com. I will discuss the details of the stores I use. You may also want to research other online store platforms for your own use before committing to one.

Selling On Highwire
Highwire provides a platform for you to build an online store. You can choose from several preset graphics to give your store the look you want. You can insert your logo.

To build your store you create categories and products. For each item, you can upload multiple pictures and have multiple variants. An example of variants might be knobs that you offer in chrome, gold, or black. Each variant can have its own price and associated picture. Adding items to the store is fairly straightforward. It steps you through the process.

Highwire allows you to accept Paypal and credit card payments in the shopping cart portion. It will also calculate shipping for customers before checkout.

If you choose to ship overseas, you can also choose which countries you want to ship to.

Highwire only charges a monthly flat fee of $29.95 at the time of this writing. They do not collect a commission on your sales, so your maximum out of pocket is the monthly fee.

You can find more information at www.highwire.com

Selling on Reverb.com
Reverb.com is similar to eBay except it is strictly for buying and selling musical products. Individuals and businesses can list items. You can list items as fixed pricing or auctions. When

listing an item, you can choose to allow people to make offers on items if you so desire.

At the time of this writing, Reverb.com takes 3.5% of the total of the sale price and shipping charges. There is, however a $1 minimum fee for items sold. This would come into effect for listing with a total of less than $29. There is a maximum fee of $350 for items over $10,000.

They do offer a "Bump" option for an additional charge. You can purchase 1,000 bumps of a product for $7.00. This means that Reverb.com will put your product at the top of their home page up to 1,000 times or until it sells. If that item does not sell after 1,000 bumps, it costs you nothing. Bumps are also pro-rated. If it sells after 100 bumps, your bump fee is only $.70.

Comparisons
Comparing my online stores, here is how they differ and the advantages and disadvantages of each. I must tell you that I have only been on Reverb.com for a short while, but I made my first sale within 24 hours of launching my store.

Comparing the three, I have made the most money on eBay. They have millions of users all over the world. When looking for unique items, people, including myself, search eBay. The feedback and rating system helps keep people honest and encourages sellers to provide prompt shipping and offer good customer service to maintain high ratings. People may feel more comfortable paying a higher price for the same item from a seller with high feedback ratings than a lower price from someone with lots of negative feedback. eBay also offers buyer and seller protection.

I set up my Highwire store, Guitar Upgrades Online, in order to save money on fees and to have a website where someone may "Google" "guitar upgrades" and be directed to my store. The big difference in this is if someone lands on my store, there is no competition there. All of the listings are mine, so people might order pickups, knobs, and a wiring kit. It has had high and low months, but the cost is only $29.95 per month. As long as I make enough sales on this website to keep the monthly fee lower than what I would pay eBay for the same amount of sales, I will keep that store up. The disadvantage of a website like this, is that it is up to you to make people aware that it exists. The key is to drive store traffic and have items that people want to purchase. It's just another place where my business is present on the web.

Reverb.com is my newest online store venture. You can go there and search AM Guitar Works to find my store. Its advantages are lower selling fees than eBay and it is focused solely on music products. It doesn't have as many users as eBay because it is strictly focused on music. It is a newer site, though, and is growing in popularity amongst people who buy and sell music gear. Since there are no monthly fees, all it costs to start is the time to get your products listed.

Summary
Selling online can be a great revenue source. It allows you to generate income 24 hours a day, seven days a week, 365 days a year. It seems like lots of purchases are made late at night or in the wee hours of the morning. We call it making money while we sleep.

My iPad has an app that makes a "cha-ching" cash register sound whenever someone makes a purchase on our eBay store. It's cool to be sitting back, watching TV in the evening and hear a signal letting you know that you have more money than you did a few seconds ago. You just made money in the guitar biz!

Chapter 7

Retail Guitar Store

There are opportunities to make money in the guitar biz with retail stores. However, proceed with caution. Don't read this book, go out and rent retail space, order a bunch of guitars and amps and sit and wait for people to come in and buy them. You really need to have a plan and educate yourself on retail. Do your homework. There are entire books written on the subject of owning a retail business. I suggest you read at least one or two of those. The purpose of this book is to share my experience and knowledge as it relates to the guitar business.

What we are going to focus on mainly in this chapter is finding a location and getting inventory to stock your store. We will also talk about how AM Guitar Repair transitioned from a repair and lesson business to AM Guitar Works, a full blown guitar retail shop.

Almost everything discussed in this book so far can be done out of your home. In order to do a significant amount of retail sales, you need to have a "brick and mortar" store.

I got into guitar retail sales gradually, but halfway through writing this book, I greatly expanded the retail portion of my business which gives me more information to share with you.

I was giving guitar lessons when I started my repair business in my home. One of my parts suppliers was Mighty Mite, which is part of Westheimer Corp. They also carry Cort guitars and basses.

Since I was a guitar teacher, people would always ask me what kind of guitar they should get. Now that I was a dealer, I could sell them a Cort guitar and then give them lessons.

Prior to that, I would take them guitar shopping at local stores. I usually kept a new acoustic guitar in stock to sell. I didn't have a showroom full of guitars, but it was nice supplementing my income with the very occasional guitar sale.

My first commercial location was not ideal for a retail guitar store, so I was still doing mainly lessons and repairs and selling guitars occasionally. My business was located in an old school building with no outdoor signage. It was hidden away in an area of town which was not very busy. The building sat up on a hill and looked kind of run down. The rent, however, was very affordable. AM Guitar Repair was a "destination" shop, which means people had to know about my business in order to find it.

One day the landlord came by and announced to all the tenants that the building was being sold and was going to be converted into residential condos, so we had to look for new locations.

I decided since I was being forced to move, I might as well make the best of the situation and saw it as an opportunity to expand the retail portion of the business. I knew that wherever I moved, the rent would be higher so I needed a way to bring more money into the business.

You will want to work with a realtor experienced in commercial properties once you decide to make the move. I am not a real estate expert, but I can share what I've learned from experience and talking to other business owners. Your realtor will be able to help you through the process, but the more knowledge you have in the subject, the better equipped you will be to get the best location. The realtor is working for you *and* the landlord. *You* are the one who needs to have your best interest in mind.

Location, Location, Location
"When choosing a retail spot, the three most important things are location, location, and location".

"Looking for a place in a great location, that is spacious, and affordable? Pick two".

I say this with a sense of humor but there is a lot of truth in these two statements. Our location in the old school building was spacious and affordable, but not a great retail location. Our next location sacrificed space for high visibility and affordability.

What to Consider In a Retail Location
- Visibility – Signage, amount of street traffic
- Convenience – Parking, Wheelchair Access
- Size of Space
- Affordability
- Security for your property, customers and employees

Visibility
When you are in the retail business you want people to find you, even if they aren't looking for you. Ideally, you want to be in a high traffic area with signage that is easily seen.

I moved the business to its current location which is in a strip mall near a busy intersection in town. It is easy to get to from the interstate. We have signage on the street as well as on our storefront. The "anchor" of the strip mall is a popular restaurant and sports bar which does a good business. At lunch time, happy hour, and dinner time, the parking lot fills up and we get some walk-in business from that. We also have a busy hair salon and a furniture store in the strip mall and have had a few walk-ins from their customers as well.

When we moved we started working with a PR firm. We changed the name of the business from AM Guitar Repair to AM Guitar Works. We wanted a more encompassing name since we planned to expand the retail portion of our business. Our PR firm designed a new logo, signage, and website for us.

I told the logo designer that I wanted a sign that would catch a guitar player's eye, and something that symbolized and showed we handled electric and acoustic guitars. You can see our logo on our website. This has worked really well on our street sign. I have been told by several people, "I was driving by and saw the sign and turned around."

As long as we're talking about visibility, let's discuss the storefront. You want it to attract attention and look professional. We are fortunate to have lots of windows on our storefront. Most music stores have their repair shops and lesson areas hidden away in the back. We chose to do something different. Our lesson studio is in one of the front windows. Our repair shop is also located and visible through the front windows.

Since lessons and repairs were, and still are the majority of profit in our business, we wanted to let people know about it. It also happened to work out the way that the space was configured when we moved in. Having the repair shop in the front window, where they can see us working on guitars shows that we are knowledgeable. Having the lesson studio in the front window has gained us lots of new students. People going to the restaurant or the hair salon next to us see people taking lessons and it sparks their interest.

Convenience
Everyone is in a hurry these days so being in a convenient location is a plus. Having ample parking spaces and being easy to get to will benefit your business. Wheelchair access is important as well.

Size and Space
When looking at retail space, you have to determine several things. If you get too small a space, you may outgrow it quickly, which sounds like a good problem to have, but moving is expensive and time consuming. If you get a space that gives you room to grow, there are risks involved as well. If the space is too big, you risk it looking empty if you can't afford to fill it with inventory. Also, more space means more money and it can drag your business down financially if you aren't quickly able to grow into it.

One possibility if you are getting more space than you need is to check with the owner to see if you can sub-lease part of the space. Another idea, since you're in the guitar business, is to convert part of the space to lesson studios and charge rent to instructors. This brings in more store traffic.

You also have to see if the interior layout of the building is set up properly for your business. If it is not, will the landlord let you modify it? You need to consider the cost of any remodeling that will be necessary.

When we moved to our current location, the only thing we did was to cut out a window in the room which is now our repair shop. The reception desk is on one side of the window and we have a checkout counter on the other side of the window. We also painted the walls and installed slatwall to hang guitars on.

Affordability

Before entering into a retail business, you will need to have a business plan. Your business plan will help you determine what you can afford.

How much money you are going to make in business is going to have several determining factors which we will discuss in the Business Strategies section of this book.

Something to keep in mind is that you do not necessarily have to pay the asking price for rental. Things are negotiable. In the city where we are located there are lots of retail spaces for rent. Some of them have been on the market for quite some time. If you're thinking of opening a retail store, start scoping out locations that will be suitable. The longer a location has been on the market, the more the landlord may be willing to work with you. They are losing money on a building that is sitting empty.

Security

When choosing a location, you want to make sure you're not in a high crime area. Theft and property damage are expensive. You want to be in an area where you, your customers, and employees will feel safe.

No matter where you are, you will want to have a security system with an alarm. We were fortunate enough that there was an existing security system built in to our location. All we have to pay for is the monthly fee. A security system may consist of door sensors, window break sensors, motion sensors, and security cameras. Check with your local security companies.

Also, make sure you have good locks and that you have the locks changed when you move in. Your landlord may do this, or you may have to do it, but it is well worth it. You never know who might have a key to your door.

You Found A Space, Now What?

Once you find a space, you need to iron out the details between you, your realtor and the landlord. There is a document called a "Letter of Intent" or LOI. The LOI is a document that you submit stating that you intend to lease the location. The document may contain any modifications that you want to make to the property and who will pay for the remodeling. The LOI is also where you make an offer on the lease rates and conditions.

Keep in mind the Letter of Intent is not a legal and binding document. Just because it is in writing does not mean that everything on the LOI is going to happen.

Signing A Lease

The lease IS a legal and binding document. Make sure you read it thoroughly and understand it. I highly recommend you hire an attorney to help with this. I also highly recommend that everything you think is true is written into the lease. Examples of what should be in the lease are the amount of square footage included, any modifications that you will be making and paying for, any modifications the landlord will make and pay for, and who is paying for utilities.

Keep in mind that it doesn't matter what the spec sheet or the Letter of Intent says. It doesn't matter what you were verbally told. None of these are legal, binding documents.

The lease, however, is legal and binding. So anything that is in the spec sheet, letter of intent, or anything you have verbally agreed on should be written into the lease. I cannot stress this enough. I will say it again. Use a reputable realtor and an attorney. Remember, *you* are the only one who has your best interests in mind.

Stocking Your Store

If you are going to own a retail guitar store, you're going to need inventory to sell. So how do you choose what products to carry? You need to do your homework here. Are you the only guitar shop in town? What brands do your competitors carry? What is popular? What will sell and make a profit for you?

My recommendation is to carry brands that your competition does not carry. In fact, you may not be able to carry some of the same brands as your local competitors. I contacted a rep for a brand that I wanted to carry. I was unable to get that brand because another local music store stocks and has carried that brand for several years. Out of courtesy, they do not allow another dealership to be in the same city.

You want brands with good name recognition. People want to buy something they have heard of or read about. You also want to have a wide variety of price ranges. You will want at least to have entry level and mid-range guitars. You may also want to carry some higher end guitars as well. Again, it depends on what is available and marketable in your particular area and the clientele you are focused on. Our best-selling models of guitars are in the $250 - $400 range. We stock some lower priced and some higher priced guitars as well. Many times we can use the lower priced items to sell the higher priced ones as people can see, feel, and hear the difference.

Distributors have varying dealer requirements such as minimum purchase. Some brands may even dictate what your initial order will be. In most cases, the more you purchase, the lower your cost per item will be.

Once you have chosen a brand, before you place the initial order, it's a good idea to try to pre-sell some of the items. If you already have musician friends, family, students or repair customers, let them know you are going to be ordering. Ask for pre-payment if possible. This will help pay for the initial order, lowering your cost to get the dealership.

Setting Up New Guitars
If you are going to sell guitars, I highly recommend you go through the guitars as they come in. Most of the time, guitars need set up even when they are new. This is one of the ways we

differentiate our business from our competition. Depending on the level of guitars that you are selling, they sometimes arrive with issues. These issues are usually things that can be taken care of quickly if you're familiar with guitar setup and minor repairs. Usually the truss rod needs adjustment. Sometimes the nut slots need a little filing. We've been told that we have the best playing guitars in town. We advertise this and use it as a selling point to differentiate our business from others.

I've had customers who came from a competitor disappointed because the $1500 guitar they tried out didn't feel good. High action, sharp fret ends, etc. I end up selling them a $400 guitar that plays great and feels good because it has been properly set up. The competitor lost a $1500 sale because they neglected to set the guitar up properly. This is called value added service.

Used Gear
People are always looking for used guitars, amps and related gear. I always welcome trade-ins. I have also purchased "fixer-upper" guitars and amps and done the repairs necessary to get them into shape. Sometimes you can find these at pawn shops. In my experience, if you purchase multiple items, they will deal with you.

This can be very profitable if you are good at repairs. Sometimes they just need a good cleaning, some new strings, and setup to be showroom ready. Our part time employee does a lot of this type of work.

Consignment
I have done some consignment sales. I am picky about what items I will sell on consignment, though. I will only take an item

on consignment if I think it will sell fairly quickly. Our showroom space is limited. If I fill it up with other peoples' items, I have less room for my own.

Should you decide to sell items on consignment, make sure you are getting a decent commission. Typical consignment rates are anywhere from 20-40%. Some people balk at these rates, but for every square foot their item takes up, you lose those square feet that you could put items that make you 50% markup.

Another thing I've found is many times people think their item is worth more than what it will actually sell for. They may say, "I need to get $400 for it and you can keep anything above that." I explain that it doesn't work that way. The truth may be that the item might only sell for $300 and if the commission is 30%, they will get $210 and I will get $90. Meanwhile, that item was taking up space where I could have put a similarly priced item and made $150 in profit.

You need to have a consignment agreement written up and have the customer sign it. The agreement I use states that I can call the customer at my discretion and have them pick up their item if it hasn't sold. They may also pick up their item at any time if they find another buyer or change their mind about selling it.

Selling on consignment can be profitable if done correctly. The main thing is to pick and choose what you will take on consignment and be sure to charge a high enough percentage so that you make a worthwhile amount of money for your time and showroom space.

Accessories

Accessories are a must for a guitar shop. When someone purchases a guitar there are lots of items that can be sold along with it, especially if it is someone's first guitar. You will want to carry cases, straps, cables, capos, picks, strings, tuners, books, etc. This will increase your profits on the sale. People expect to be able to buy these types of things at a guitar shop. We get most of our accessories and books from Harris-Teller. Not only do they carry guitar accessories, they carry all types of musical instruments and accessories including band and orchestra instruments.

Setting Up Your Showroom

The look of your store is important. Your showroom should be well-lit, clean and organized. Decide on a color scheme for your store. Go to other guitar shops and check out their showrooms. Figure out what you like or don't like about them. Always have cables and picks handy, as well as chairs or stools for people to sit while they try out guitars.

There are several ways to display guitars. The most common way is on hooks on slatwall. Slatwall can be purchased at building material stores such as Menard's. It comes in 4' x 8' sheets. It's usually white, but can be painted. When we set up our store, we cut the slatwall into 1 foot wide strips and cut the lengths to fit our walls. Another option to slat wall is wire slat grid panels. These are lighter weight than slatwall and use the same hooks.

You will need guitar hooks as well. Make sure to get sturdy hooks. At one point, we ordered some lower priced hooks online. Some of them were fine, but others were poorly welded and looked like they were going to break with the weight of the heavier guitars and basses. You don't want to damage a guitar because you were stingy on the hooks.

Pegboard works great for hanging accessories such as strings, cables and other accessories. Pegboard can also be purchased and cut to different sizes. You can make a frame out of 1" x 2" lumber and attach it to the wall. Then mount the pegboard to the frame. The hooks for pegboard are very inexpensive and come in a variety of lengths and configurations.

Display cases are a must. These are great for displaying items that don't fit on pegboard or slatwall. They are also more secure and many come with locks to prevent theft. They can be used as a counter or room divider as well.

Most startup businesses don't have a lot of money to spend on store fixtures. Getting used store fixtures is usually not a problem. Check out Craigslist or office furniture stores who carry used furniture and fixtures.

Hiring Employees
If you are opening a retail store, it is possible to be a one person operation. Hopefully your business grows to the point that you will need to hire someone, or even a few people to work for you. Hiring the right people is the key to the success of a business. Hiring the wrong person can be devastating to your business.

Before hiring someone, figure out what they will be doing. Write a job description. Then figure out what skills are necessary and most important for the type of work. Most small businesses need people who are able to cover several duties. If you're running a guitar shop, someone with knowledge of guitars and music is pretty important.

They should interact well with people and have sales skills. They should also be enthusiastic and have good customer skills. The "feel" of a store has a lot to do with the people who work there.

As a consumer you can take note of your experiences in stores that you shop in. Make visits to your competitors occasionally to see what they are doing.

The first employee I hired happens to be my daughter, Brianna. She is creative, excellent with customers in person and on the phone. She is very organized and neat (which complements my shortcomings in this area). I brought her onboard when we moved to the new location. She works mainly during the time I am giving lessons. That way I don't have to interrupt a lesson to wait on customers.

She answers the phone, keeps an eye on the store, and ships all the items we sell online. She also does some of the basic maintenance items on guitars as well. She polishes frets, oils fingerboards, restrings guitars, and cleans and polishes them. By having her do all these things, it frees me up to do more advanced work.

Hiring a family member can be a good thing if they have the skills and traits needed for the job. Also, a family member may take more interest in the business, especially if they are still living at home. You're always giving your kids money anyway, why not make it tax deductible by having them on your payroll?

However, hiring a family member could also cause problems if they are not a good fit. If you have to fire them, that puts you and the family member in an awkward situation. Make sure they are qualified and fit the job requirements.

Hire someone with skills that complement yours. You might be a great guitar tech, teacher, or salesperson. You might be lousy at organization, creativity, or social media marketing. What areas are you lacking in that would benefit your business?

One of the other hires I recently made is someone who has been one of my guitar students for several years. Shelley is a high school student and is excited about guitars. She even completed my Guitar Building 101 class.

She is mechanically inclined and is able to do basic setups and minor repairs. She works during the times I am giving lessons, so she is generating repair revenue during that time as well.

There are lots of tax laws involved with hiring people. There are differences between hiring your own family members when they are under 18 years of age vs. hiring employees who are not family members. Work with an accountant to make sure you are correctly withholding and paying taxes correctly.

Summary
This chapter has only scratched the surface of the information you need to know when opening a retail business. There will be more information in upcoming chapters that you can apply to a retail store as well. However, educate yourself. There are entire books dedicated to the subjects in this chapter. I recommend *The*

Complete Idiot's Guide to Starting and Running a Retail Store.
It gives you a lot to think about.

Opening a retail store can be a risky venture depending on the
economic climate and competition in your particular area.
Besides competing with local businesses, you are competing
with internet guitar shops as well. I'm not trying to scare you, or
talk you out of it. I just want to make sure that you look at all
the risks. I have found owning my own guitar shop to be a very
rewarding experience. I love what I do every day and I work
hard to make sure the business does well.

Chapter 8

Lesson Studio

Since we've been talking about lessons, let's take it to another level. You can make money in the guitar biz by owning and operating a lesson studio. A lesson studio can be a stand-alone business, or it can be part of a retail operation.

I interviewed Greg Hipskind, drum instructor and owner of QC Rock Academy in Davenport, IA. Greg is also the drummer for regional touring band Wicked Liz and the Bellyswirls.

QC Rock Academy has six individual lesson rooms, a front area for group classes, and a larger room for band rehearsals. They offer lessons for guitar, drums, bass, keyboard, and voice.

Greg is doing lots of cool stuff there, so I asked him to share information on how this business started, has grown, and continues to grow.

What made you decide to open a lesson studio?
Greg: It was something that had been in the back of my mind for a while. I was teaching at a music store and it closed down. Then I started teaching at a lesson studio and it shut down with only a week notice.

I had a full roster of students and no place to teach. My wife and I had been saving money for a down payment on a house. We talked and decided we would use that money to open a lesson studio.

We found a location in a mall and signed a three year lease. A few days later we found out we were going to have our first child. That was when I knew failure was not an option.

Did you have previous business experience?
Greg: The only experience I had was teaching at the other places. I knew what I liked and what I would do different than those places.

I had no experience running a business, but I read lots of books in a very short time. "EntreLeadership" by Dave Ramsey was a big inspiration to me.

What are some of the challenges involved in starting and owning a lesson studio?
Greg: The startup was the most difficult part. It took around four months from the time that the studio I was teaching at closed down until my location was open for business.

In the interim I kept most of my students by teaching at their homes. I was driving a lot, but was able to retain most of my clients.

We needed to remodel the space we leased to divide it into lesson rooms. The father of one of my students was a framing and drywall contractor, so we traded that work for lessons. I painted the walls.

Our office furniture and amplifiers were purchased at auctions. We probably spent less than $100 for furniture and equipment.

We opened in November and had our grand opening in December. It was good timing because you always get a surge in students in January after people have gotten musical instruments for Christmas.

The other challenge was not knowing if it was going to work. There are no guarantees when you open a business.

In our first year, when summer came, our student levels dropped off significantly. People were taking summers off to go to camp or vacations, etc.

What we did to address the reduction in summer students the following year was to start music camps. We do vocal camps, guitar camp, and band performance camps.

How are the instructors paid, and how does the studio generate income for the owner?
Greg: Our instructors are private contractors. They are not employees. The students pay the instructors directly. Each month the instructors pay me 20% of each lesson they were paid for. I also have my own roster of students that pay me directly.

What marketing strategies do you use?
Greg: We use social media, word of mouth, and Craigslist. We've also gotten coverage from local media outlets such as the newspaper and TV news. We don't pay for advertising. We've tried radio and newspaper ads and neither one have generated enough business to justify the cost.

How do students find you?
Greg: Most students find us through referrals and through the marketing previously mentioned.

How do you differentiate your business from others who provide music lessons?
Greg: We focus only on rock instruments – guitar, drums, bass, keyboard and vocals. We provide a fun, energetic environment. We offer performance classes where we group students into bands. We don't just teach people to sing or play their instruments. We are coaching kids how to actually perform. Our vocal students learn how to handle a microphone. We are teaching artist development.

We also allow the kids to interact with well-known artists via "meet and greets" with bands when they come into town to perform. We've met Florida Georgia Line, Shinedown, Zach Brown Band, Alice in Chains, Cheap Trick and more.

We've scheduled Skype sessions with celebrity musicians including Rudy Sarzo, (bassist for Quiet Riot and Dio), and Bruce Kulick (Kiss).

What do you enjoy most about owning your own business?
Greg: I set my own hours. I don't have to answer to a boss. I also enjoy the fulfillment of seeing my own work be successful.

What advice would you offer to someone interested in opening a lesson studio?
Greg: Find good quality instructors. Do background checks. Put out a good quality product. Get to know all the students and their parents. Never stop trying to get your name out. Always work to keep the kids and parents excited about it. Do research on your competition. Avoid debt and be smart about how you manage money.

Chapter 9

Group Classes

There are opportunities to make money in the guitar biz with group classes. If you know how to do something that other people want to learn, you can make money teaching them.

At AM Guitar Works we have done guitar building, pedal building, and tube amplifier building classes. We have also done group ukulele lessons and guitar maintenance classes.

Teaching group classes was something that I thought of during the planning stages of starting my business. I was especially inspired when I attended a weekend fretwork class in Chicago. The class was $525 and included 6 feet of fret wire, lunch, and the instruction. There were 10 people in the class, so they made over $5000 that weekend. For me, it was well worth the price because I learned skills that I needed in order to pursue my guitar repair career.

Group classes can be very profitable because you are having multiple people pay you for your time simultaneously. It also gets you in front of several people all at once.

Let's start with something simple. I partnered with a local lesson studio to do group ukulele lessons. We've done them in January or February so that everyone who got a uke for Christmas and didn't know how to play, could sign up. It's a one hour class and I teach the students four songs. We take up to 10 people in a class and charge $15. I get $10 for each student and the lesson studio gets $5 for every student.

It took some time to get the curriculum and the visual aids together for the first class, but now I can do it with very little prep time. Both the lesson studio and AM Guitar Works promote the class. I also bring merchandise to the class such as electronic tuners, cases, books, etc. People usually buy something extra to take home. They also get business cards and many times show up at my shop for more goodies.

My first series of classes were Guitar Building 101 classes. They have been very popular. It's a weekend class and we use pre-finished bodies and necks. These are not pre-made kits. I came up with the parts list through trial and error with parts from multiple vendors. The students get to pick their own color schemes, type of neck, pickups, etc.

In the class we assemble the guitars. The critical routing and some of the drilling for the neck screws in the body is already done. We drill the necessary holes, assemble the guitars, and wire the electronics. Finally, we set them up to play great.

I have had people come from all over to take the class including Canada, and Puerto Rico.

This class starts at $699 with several additional options that can be added on. Some of the options that we offer for an upcharge include quilted or flamed maple tops, higher quality pickups, gloss lacquered neck, and sparkle finishes. $300 of the class is billed as tuition and the rest is for parts, from which we also make a profit.

The next class I added was a Pedal Building Class. I get the kits from Mojo Musical Supply and MOD Kits DIY. This is a one day class. My fee for the class is $100 plus the pedal kit, which I make a little profit on as well.

Some people are interested in just building the kits themselves without taking the class. I tell them the advantages to taking the class are that they get to hear other pedals, and I guarantee they end up with a working pedal. I am happy to sell them a kit to put together on their own if they are still not interested in taking the class.

My most recent class is a Tube Amp Building class. We build five watt tube amps from MOD Kits DIY. They are great sounding amps and they are fairly easy to assemble. They are simple circuit amps with Bass, Treble, and Volume controls. The amp is housed in a steel chassis with the tubes and the transformers sitting on top. They can be connected to a speaker cabinet which is not included. I do sell speaker cabinets as an option.

Students who take the class can use the amp as is. It's got a boutique look to it. Or they can build or buy their own cabinet to house the amp. One of my students installed it in an antique radio cabinet. We put a 3.5mm jack on it so an MP3 player could be connected to it. He can listen to his favorite tunes through an antique radio.

Early on, I feared that by teaching people the "tricks of the trade", I would be training my competition. However, it has been quite the opposite. The people who have been in my guitar, amp, and pedal building classes have become some of my best customers. When you spend a couple days with people you get to know them. You're able to let them know what other products and services you offer. I have several students who have done multiple classes. One of the Guitar Building 101 class students is now an employee at AM Guitar Works.

Some of the group classes I've done have been at no charge. Sometimes it pays off just to get in front of a group of people who may not know about your business. I recently did presentation for a "guitar camp" being conducted at a local lesson studio. The camp was four hours per day over a five day period. They invited guest guitarists to come in and show the group various styles of playing. They also had a guest demo his pedalboard so the students could learn what pedals do and how to dial in tones.

Being in the repair business, we did a guitar maintenance class. We showed the students how to polish frets, oil a fingerboard, tighten the tuning key hardware, clean and polish the guitar, and how to change strings. These were kids age 12-18. I did the class at no charge, but because I got in front of these kids, I picked up some repair business and future customers to my store. We, of course, handed out flyers and coupons while we were there.

Summary
Here is what I recommend to make money doing group classes:
- Figure out what you can do that others want to learn and set up a class
- Take opportunities to get in front of people who are potential customers

- Have options that can be added on or purchased before, during, or after the class
- If you have an online store, set up a class registration that can be purchased online. Post links to the registration on social media.

Chapter 10
Guitar Building

There are opportunities to make money if you are good at building guitars. Since I am not an expert in the guitar building business, I contacted some builders that I have met through networking and asked them to share their expertise. Each one of them is in different stages of their guitar building career.

The first interview is with Doug Kauer, owner of Kauer guitars in Elk Grove, CA. I got to know Doug through the Reranch guitar forum.

How did you get started building guitars?
Doug: My dad owns a cabinet shop and I worked for him. I've been around woodworking forever. My wife's family is all musicians. My father-in-law did instrument repair work. I think he was waiting for my brain to realize that I am a woodworker and I should be building guitars. One day, a piece of wood came into the shop and I thought it would make a nice guitar. I got parts to build the guitar as a birthday gift, but I never finished it. During the process of building it, I learned things that I should have done different. I started over and it was down the rabbit hole from there. I started building my own designs and people started buying them. It just kind of grew from there.

How do people find out about your guitars?
Doug: Many people find us online, mostly through social media. We use Facebook, Instagram, and Twitter. We have worked with some dealers, but have scaled way back from that.

We have built up a reputation, so we sell most guitars directly to the customer. Now that we're established, I can be a lot pickier about who I work with. Dealers were only a small percentage of our total sales.

What types of marketing or promotion do you use?
Doug: Besides social media, we have advertized in guitar magazines. We occasionally use paid advertizing to promote a post on Facebook. If I spend a few dollars and sell a $3,000 guitar, it's worth it. It's hard to tell how effective each advertizing method is, or what works best. I think it's a combination of everything we use.

Do you have any well-known musicians who are your customers?
Yes, we do. Walter Becker (Steely Dan) owns 2 Banshees and an Argonaut. Tommy Kessler (Blondie) plays Kauer guitars almost exclusively. Michael "Iron Man" Burks bought the second Daylighter model we ever made. Unfortunately he passed away a few years ago. He recorded his last album "Show of Strength" with a Kauer guitar. He's pictured with the guitar on the cover of that album. Scott Holiday of Rival Sons plays Kauer guitars. Rival Sons is one of my favorite bands. We also have local, regional, and studio musicians playing our guitars.

What these artists do for me is mental support. Seeing them use my guitars keeps me going. Besides helping sales, it's a reminder that we're doing it right.

As far as getting our instruments into the hands of well-known musicians, our policy is everybody pays. We don't give away guitars just to get an endorsement.

What are some your business philosophies/approaches?
Doug: I take what we do very seriously, but I don't take myself seriously. We use humor on our website and advertizing. Kauer Guitars is quirky in personality. You'll see that in our ads. Each guitar gets stamped "Made in the USA by Men with Beards and Hammers".

From a business standpoint, we are a "semi-custom" builder. What I mean is that we have certain models. We aren't like some luthiers who will build something to your sketch.

You can choose from 3 families of guitars. Each family has a few models, and you can choose several options within those models. I like to stick to certain types of woods and hardware because I know what works well for us. All of our neck-through models are made of Spanish cedar, which has a unique tone. We offer optional top woods such as redwood and quilted or flamed maple.

We make around 100 guitars per year. It's just me and one part time worker. If I had the staff we could do about 500 per year, but I enjoy being a small builder.

How do you stand out from the competition?
Doug: There are lots of small builders, but we don't necessarily consider each other competition. As long as you're building something original and unique, people will either like your guitars or someone else's. Our guitars sound different than everyone else's because of the combination of wood, hardware, and electronics we use.

You do have to be heard among the noise, though. We like to emphasize our unique aesthetics, our tone, and our sense of humor.

We also don't try to be what I call "magician builders". We don't build guitars that people look at and say, "How do they do that?" We build a great guitar with unbelievable sound and a unique look that you're not afraid to take out and play.

Do you have advice for people who are interested in building guitars?
Doug: Marry someone with a good job *(laughs)*. Don't undervalue your work. Don't tell yourself, "I'll lose money in the short run". If you want to be taken seriously, price yourself accordingly. Be original, but you don't have to be out in left field with your designs. There's a lot of wiggle room. You can carve a niche for yourself.

Always try to improve. I strive to build each guitar a little better than the last one. Stick with it and keep going. Be relentless with social media and advertizing. Keep beating people over the head until they get it. Meet other builders. Drink beer with them and talk guitars.

What's the most challenging part about the guitar building business?
Doug: You put in lots of hours building, promoting, going to guitar shows, etc. It's enjoyable, but when you calculate your hourly wage, it's pretty low.

One of the hardest things for me is to see one of my guitars for sale used. We've all bought and sold guitars, but it's hard not to take it personally.

What do you enjoy most about building guitars?
Doug: I've been lucky enough to be taken under the wings of other builders. Now I am able to help others. As long as you're a good builder and not ripping people off, everybody's willing to help out. We are a support group for each other. I love the comradery in this business. It helps to know you're not the only one that has bills to pay or has the occasional bad day. If I'm having a tough day, I'll just call up another builder and vent.

I love seeing our guitars being played. I love it when they come in after 5 years for a setup and repairs and they're beat up from being played a lot. I'm putting my name on something that I hope is going to be around for a lot longer than I am.

Kauer Guitars Info:
Website: www.kauerguitars.com
Check out "Kauer Guitars" on Facebook
Email: info@kauerguitars.com

G'Zan Custom Guitars
I also spoke with Mark Newsbaum of G'Zan Custom Guitars. Mark is another acquaintance of mine through the Reranch guitar forum.

How did you get started building guitars?
Mark: I took a class in which we built a "kit" guitar. Then I liked it so much, I built one for my son as a Christmas gift. It turned out so well, that I got into doing it as a hobby. I had always tinkered with them, doing my own setups and adjustments and also worked on my friends guitars. But that's what got me into building them.

How do people find out about your guitars?
Mark: I do the local guitar shows and the past 2 years I have done the Dallas International Guitar Festival. I also have put them in a couple local music stores on consignment. Word of

mouth helps, too. I plan to put an ad in a couple guitar magazines in the next few months, just to see if that will work.

What types of marketing or promotion do you use?
Mark: Right now, just shows and word of mouth. I do have a few pro players who also use word of mouth to help me, as well as one endorsee who mentions me on his CD covers.

Tell me about any well-known musicians who are your customers?
Mark: Years ago I met former Robert Plant guitarist, Innes Sibun, on MySpace. We became friends, and I built a guitar for him. He's the one who promotes me on his CD's...even wrote a song called "The G'Zan Hoedown" on his latest CD, "Lost in the Wilderness". I also donated one to a charity auction that was purchased by Jim "Moose" Brown, who is a guitarist with "Bob Seger& the Silver Bullet Band". He also co-wrote the song "It's 5 o'clock Somewhere". I have several local Nashville players who play them, including Eric Lopez of the band "Coal Black Engine". I just built one for a guitarist in the Netherlands, who plays in "The Bud Spencer Rock Explosion".

What are some of your business philosophies/approaches?
Mark: I started out building guitars to give people alternatives to what factories build. For example, if you wanted a Tele style, but different pickups or fret sizes or switching options, custom colors, whatever, I can build it for you. Now, in addition to doing that kind of stuff, I am developing my OWN designs and ideas as well. I try to give people the guitar they want rather than what the corporate factories force upon us guitarists. I use only nitrocellulose lacquer, and the best components, and personally setup the guitars to the customer's specs.

Do you have advice for people who are interested in building guitars?

Mark: Learn all you can about guitar construction. Build a kit first to understand the construction and how they go together. Don't think you can get "rich". It takes years and even decades of work and failures before you get "good" at it. But most of all be passionate and enjoy the ride!! LOL!!!

G'Zan Custom Guitars, LLC.
Website www.gzancustomguitars.com

Thank you to Doug and Mark for sharing their knowledge and experience. Good luck in your future guitar building endeavors. I hope you continue to enjoy making money in the guitar biz.

Part II – Small Business Strategies

Part I of this book was dedicated to giving you ideas for generating revenue in the guitar business. Part II of the book is going to discuss small business strategies. Most of these strategies are not unique to the guitar business, and can be applied to just about any small business. If you know "non-guitar" people who are in business or want to be, please recommend this book to them as well.

I enjoy making my living in the guitar business. Even though it's fun, it has to be taken seriously because this is how I pay my bills and put food on the table for my family. I am highly motivated to keep the business running because this is my lifelong dream. There is nothing else that I would rather do than spend time selling, repairing and teaching people to play the guitar. In order to keep things rolling, you need to continually educate yourself on business strategies. The world and technology that is available to you are constantly changing. It is important to learn the terminology and current technology. Whatever business you're in, whether it is guitar-related or something else, make sure you are staying up to date on what's hot and what's not.

This book is meant to be an overview. For each chapter of my book, you can probably find hundreds of books written on that subject. Don't make this the only one you read before quitting your day job to start your own business. The main reason I wrote this book is because I saw a niche. There are tons of books about business and tons of books about guitars, but nothing that ties it all together. There are also many business and entrepreneur blogs on the internet.

So let's get started discussing small business strategies!

Chapter 11
Business Basics – Making It Official

Making money with guitars is fun, but if you want to start and run a business, there is work involved. There are some basic steps you need to take to make your business official. You need to get a sales tax license for your state. This gets you set up to collect and pay sales tax. You need to know the rates for your area. Does your county have a local option sales tax?

You also need to know what is taxable and non-taxable. In Iowa, musical instrument repair labor is non-taxable. Music lessons are also non-taxable in Iowa. However, if you repair an amplifier or other electronic accessory that is not an actual instrument, that labor is taxable. In Iowa, you can pay sales tax you've collected online monthly, quarterly, or annually. No matter how often you choose to pay, make sure to put the sales tax money aside so you are able to pay it on time and avoid penalties. Check with your state's website for tax rates, what is taxable, and how to pay.

Choosing and Registering Your Business Name
Another step you may need to take is registering your business name. In Iowa, this involves filling out a form with the business name you want to register and turning it in to the county recorder's office. They check to make sure no other Iowa businesses are using the name you have chosen. Once it's

approved it protects your business name from being duplicated by other Iowa businesses.

Choosing a good business name is important. It can help people know what you do. If you choose a generic name like "John Doe Enterprises" that doesn't really tell anyone what business you're in. When my business started, I chose "AM Guitar Repair" – my initials and what I did. At that time I was mainly focused on repairs and lessons. If people "Googled""guitar repair Quad Cities" (or any of the names of the cities), AM Guitar Repair filled the first several pages of the search results. This helped grow my business.

The problem with the name was that it was very limiting as the business expanded into more than just repair. I decided to change the name to AM Guitar Works. This was more encompassing and also allows for future expansion. Fortunately, I was able to time the name change along with relocating to a new address. I had to buy new signage and business cards anyway, so why not change the name?

Again, I am only familiar with the registration procedures I had to do. It is going to vary from state to state so be sure to do your research.

Business Bank Accounts
You will also want to open a business checking account at your bank. This will allow you to keep your business money separate from your personal account. For small businesses you can open a DBA account (Doing Business As). Your bank can help you with this process. While you're at it, open a business savings

account as well. You can use that account to set aside money for paying sales and quarterly self-employment taxes.

Business Entities - Sole Proprietorship vs. LLC
When starting any business you will need to decide whether you want to be a sole proprietor or a corporation such as LLC (Limited Liability Corporation).

In most cases, if you are starting up, a sole proprietorship is fine. It is the easiest and has the lowest cost. All you have to do is make sure you have the proper licenses and start doing business. All profit from the business is considered your personal income and that is how you are taxed. You also need to be aware that you are personally liable for any debt or lawsuits that the business may incur. Your personal assets such as your home and bank accounts can be used to satisfy unpaid debts and legal liabilities such as lawsuits.

An LLC or Limited Liability Corporation involves more paperwork and a higher startup cost. You will want to seek professional help with getting this set up should you decide to go this route. An LLC is considered a separate legal entity with its own assets and liabilities. You are not putting your personal property at risk, only the money that is invested in the LLC.

However, if you take out a loan for your LLC, but personally guarantee it, you are still personally liable for that debt. If you personally cause harm to someone in the course of business, you can still be held liable for that as well. While an LLC may offer more protection of personal assets than a sole proprietorship, you can still be held personally responsible for these types of things.

There are lots of books and articles on the internet regarding what type of business entity you should use. I highly recommend you research and assess your risk level in making this decision.

Summary
Starting a small business is not that difficult. It's keeping it going that is the challenging part. Do your research and get the proper licenses and you're on your way to making money in the guitar biz.

Chapter 12
Business Basics – Accounting

Keeping Track of It All

Once you start a business, you will need to keep track of your revenue, expenses, inventory, sales tax, and profits. You need to keep accurate records of all of your business transactions.

At AM Guitar Works we use Quickbooks software. This reasonably priced accounting software is loaded with features and will allow your business to grow into it. It lets you generate sales receipts, invoices, and checks. You can track inventory and even set it up to alert you when it's time to re-order items. I am going to base this chapter on Quickbooks because it's what I know and use. There are other accounting packages available, but the terms still apply.

Quickbooks generates all kinds of reports that let you know how your business is doing. This comes in handy at tax time. At the end of the year I print a report and take it to my accountant who uses it to figure my taxes.

You can use some of the reports in Quickbooks to see which portions of your business are profitable and which are not. You can also look at trends in your business. Are there months where revenue is lower than others that you need to prepare for?

Quickbooks has its own built in tutorials for each of its features and I highly recommend you watch the tutorials and figure out how to use it.

Accounting Terminology

You don't have to be an accountant to run a business, but as a business owner, you do need to know the terminology and concepts. Here are some accounting terms with which you need to become familiar.

Revenue

Revenue is all the money coming in from your customers. When people pay you for repairs, lessons, instruments or parts, you are collecting revenue.

Cost of Goods (COGs)

Cost of Goods is what it costs you for an item you sell. If you pay $300 for a guitar from a supplier, that is your cost of goods.

Expenses

Expenses are the costs of running your business that are not items that you resell. Examples would be rent, utilities, internet service, shipping, tools, office supplies, payroll, professional fees and travel expenses. Be sure to track all your business related expenses. If I make a business purchase, I enter the receipt as soon as I get to the computer. If you forget to enter that $75 printer cartridge as an expense, that money will be counted as income because it will not have been subtracted from your total revenue. You will pay income tax on that $75 even though you spent it on the business, because you didn't record it.

Profit

Profit = Revenue minus Cost of Goods minus Expenses. In other words what is left over after the cost of merchandise and expenses are subtracted.

Sales Tax

Sales tax is money that you collect on taxable items and services that goes to the state and county where you are doing business.

Quickbooks automatically calculates the sales tax on invoices and sales receipts based on how you set it up. It keeps track of how much you have collected. When it's time to pay the sales tax you generate a report that shows how much you owe and the numbers that you need to enter when paying it online.

Sales Receipts and Invoices

Sales receipts are what you use when you are going to collect the full payment at the time of the sale. When someone comes in and purchases an item and pays for it, we generate a sales receipt.

Invoices are for transactions where you are going to collect partial payments or you are providing a product or service that is going to be paid at a later date. For example, a customer wants to make payments to purchase a $500 guitar. You generate an invoice for the full amount. If they make a payment of $100, you click on Receive Payments in Quickbooks. Their balance due is $400. Every time they make a payment, you enter that amount and the software keeps track of the balance.

While we're on this subject, I let people make payments if they need to, but I don't let the merchandise leave the store until they are paid in full. For the most part, we collect payment in full at time of purchase. We have made a few exceptions, but only occasionally. A good thing about the guitar business is that people expect to pay for things at the time of service. They don't expect you to repair their guitar and send them a bill that's due in 30 days. They expect to pay when they pick it up.

We do provide products and services for some of the local schools. They ask for a quote, which we provide. If they approve the quote they send us a Purchase Order or PO. A PO is a document stating they approve a certain amount of money for a product or service. We then provide the product or service and send them an invoice. They usually pay within 30 days.

Gross Profit Percentage (GP%)
GP% = Income/Revenue x 100. This is a good indicator of how your business is doing. Let's say in a month you generate $10,000 in revenue. Your COG's were $3,500 and your expenses were $2,000. Your total costs are $5,500. That gives you a profit or income of $4,500. $4,500 divided by $10,000 =.45. Multiply that times 100 to get the percentage. Your GP% is 45% is the Gross Profit Percentage.

Work With an Experienced Accountant
Even though Quickbooks and other accounting programs help keep track of everything, I highly recommend you work with an experienced CPA who is familiar with small business and self-employment taxes.

Once you hire employees, this becomes even more important, as you may have questions on taxes. I send my employees' time cards to my accountant quarterly. She fills out the forms, e-mails them to me, and I submit them along with payment to the United States Treasury, State of Iowa, or wherever they need to go.

Talk to other business owners for recommendations if you don't have an accountant. You also want an accountant who is experienced at working with small businesses and those who are self-employed. Just going to one of the big tax preparer franchises may not do the trick. A good CPA will be familiar with the ever-changing tax codes and will hopefully save you money. They may also be able to make recommendations to save you money on your tax bill. Taxes are a necessity and responsibility, but the more tax you pay, the less money you have to reinvest in the business.

There have been times where we have received letters from the IRS because we changed the way we paid some of our employment taxes. We sent a payment and they did not know how to apply it. It's times like this where I am grateful to have an accountant who understands and knows how to deal with these things, so I can focus on running my business.

Tax Coaches
Awhile back I participated in a webinar that was hosted by a tax coach. Most people, like myself in the past, take all their information to their accountant once a year at tax time and hope for the best. This is like driving while all the time looking in the rear view mirror.

A tax coach will analyze your business and make recommendations before tax time so that you can legally run your business with a lower tax bill. Large companies have accountants who manage this for them. Small business owners, unless they are CPA's, are probably not familiar with the tax codes and don't know the "loop holes" to save money. Studies show that billions of dollars are paid in taxes every year that could be avoided. Again, pay what you owe, but no more than what you owe.

Self-Employment Taxes

Regular employees, which are the majority of the population, have taxes taken out of their paychecks automatically. When you are self-employed, you are required to pay estimated taxes quarterly. Do not avoid this. Doing so will cause you to end up with a huge tax bill and penalties come April 15. See your accountant for recommended amounts based on your income. I put money in a savings account on a weekly basis so it is there quarterly when it is time to pay.

Employees and Taxes

When your business grows and you add employees, things get more complicated. You will have to withhold FICA, Medicare, Federal and State taxes from their paychecks. Then you have to pay it throughout the year. Again, this is something I have my accountant handle for me. I send employee time cards to her and she e-mails me the paperwork and amounts to pay.

Inventory Management

Quickbooks has reports that can help you manage your inventory. Your inventory level needs to be kept under control. Depending on how far you go with your business, whether you're just doing repairs or have a full retail shop, managing your on hand inventory can be a critical factor in the success or failure of your business.

When you're in a retail business, you need to have a well-stocked store. People are more likely to buy if they have several choices and can put their hands on the product. If you're in the repair business, you need to have a good supply of often used parts.

Having too much inventory can be dangerous as well. If you have a lot of items that are not selling, that is known as high overhead. If you go deep in debt and overstock your store, and things don't sell, it's difficult to pay the debt down, and you can get into financial trouble.

I often use a Quickbooks report called "Sales By Item". You can set a specific date range and see how many of each item you sold. Once you have been in business for a while, you will have a good idea of what your top selling items are.

When considering ordering items, I generate a sales report that goes back a year. I look at the top selling items and see if I can get a better price on them if I order in larger quantities. If they are smaller low cost items, I order the largest quantity at the lowest price, provided I know I will go through them in less than a year.

Having said that, you need to be aware that although some items may be a top-seller this year, their popularity may wane as time goes by. A couple of years ago, ukuleles were a very hot item. They are still selling now, and I stock them, but they are not as hot as they were a couple of years ago. This year, I have seen an upward trend in banjos - mostly in repairs rather than sales. Evidently, there are still lots of banjos floating around out there from decades ago that are in need of cleaning, adjusting and general repairs. Bands like The Lumineers and Mumford and Sons have made bluegrass instruments like the banjo and mandolin more popular. Watch the trends and stock your store accordingly.

Summary

To summarize this chapter: Purchase accounting software and learn how to use it. Enter data immediately and save receipts. Make sure you work with an accountant who is experienced with self-employment and small business taxes.

Chapter 13
Accepting Payment

Methods of Accepting Payment
At AM Guitar Works we accept cash, personal checks, Paypal, and debit and credit cards.

Cash
Cash is the best type of payment in my opinion. With cash, you don't have to worry about a check bouncing, and there are no fees to pay. The only real risk is if someone tries to use counterfeit money. Counterfeit detecting pens are available at office supply stores. I highly recommend using these if someone is paying with large bills.

Personal Checks
Personal checks are my second favorite method of payment. There are no transaction fees and they can be deposited directly into your bank account so you have almost immediate access to the money.

The risk in taking personal checks, of course, is if they "bounce" due to insufficient funds. On average, I've only experienced about one bounced check per year. Of all those, I've been able to recover the money. When a check gets returned for insufficient funds, the first thing I do is call the customer. It has never been intentional in my cases. Overdrafts happen, especially on joint accounts. I always ask for cash when this happens. I also make sure to charge them for any fees I incur from my bank. If you get someone who is not responsive, you can take the returned check to their bank if it is local and ask if there is enough money in the account for the check to clear. If there is not, wait a week and try again. Friday is usually a good time to do this because a lot of people get paid on Fridays.

If the transaction is going to be a large amount and you don't know the person, or are unsure of their trustworthiness, you may want to opt for a cashier's check, cash or other form of payment.

You will need to be the judge of whether to accept personal checks in your business or not. It may depend on the area you are in or the clientele who do business with you. Some businesses no longer accept personal checks, and it has probably due to them being burned too many times.

Credit and Debit Cards
I learned early on when I went into business that having the capability to accept credit and debit cards was going to be a must. It went hand in hand with having an online store (besides eBay). Yes, you will pay fees to the merchant providing your credit card service – usually between two to three percent of the transaction amount. However, studies have shown that people will spend more money if they are putting it on plastic rather than handing over cash.

If you're just getting started, there are some smart phone devices that allow you to take credit card payments that go directly to your bank account. As your business grows, you may need something different. If you own a retail store, will customers feel secure about you or your employees swiping their card into a smart phone?

AM Guitar Works uses Propay to accept credit and debit cards. I chose them for the following reasons:

- Propay is like an online bank account, similar to Paypal.
- The money from transactions is available in your Propay account within 24 hours of the transaction taking place.
- Propay will provide you with a debit card that can be used to make purchases as long as the money is in your account.
- You can transfer money from your Propay account to your bank account. This usually takes a couple of days. Typically, it transfers quicker than Paypal in my experience.

There are a few ways that you can use Propay to collect payment. The optional card reader is the most convenient and quickest way. It attaches to your computer's USB port. You scan the customer's card, then enter the transaction amount and invoice number. The nice thing about the card reader is that you can take it offsite and connect it to a laptop to do business transactions anywhere there is an internet connection. You can also scan cards without an internet connection, but you will have to write down the information as far as amounts and invoice numbers to be entered later when you do have a connection.

You can use Propay without a card reader by filling out an online form. You have to type in the customer's name, address with city and zip code, as well as the amount and invoice number. This can be time consuming for you and the customer, but when you're first starting out, it will work. You can also use this feature if someone wants to make a credit card payment over the phone.

Another way you can use Propay is to e-mail someone a credit card invoice. You enter the amount and other information including the customer's name and email address. It sends them an email with a link to a form that they fill out. Once they've done that, the transaction is complete.

I've had customers offer to email me their credit card information and I always suggest that they not do that. You never know who might intercept it. The above mentioned method of sending them a secure email invoice is much more secure.

Propay charges an annual fee, a transaction fee and a percentage of each transaction fee. The higher the annual fee, the lower your transaction rates are. You renew annually, so before renewing make sure you are on the best plan for your business.

I urge you to look into what other options are available to you. I signed up with Propay at the start of my business. I have looked at a few other options since then and have not found one that better suits our particular business needs. However, your business needs may be different.

Your bank probably has a way for you to accept credit cards as well. I have looked into it, and still found Propay to work best for my business purposes.

Beware of the companies that call you or stop in to your business to sell credit card services. There are some that are legitimate and may be fine, but I know one small business owner who signed up for a "free trial" and ended up having to fight to get out of a contract and received billing for charges that the sales rep never mentioned.

Paypal

Paypal is the preferred method for buyers and sellers to make and receive payments on Ebay. If you have an online store people can make purchases via Paypal as well. They also offer a debit card that can be used for transactions as long as there is enough money in the account to cover the purchase. Our card has 1% cash back on all the purchases we use it for.

When someone makes a payment to you via Paypal, the money is immediately available in your account. You can leave the money in your account and use it to make purchases for your business. You can also use Paypal to purchase postage and print shipping labels. You can also transfer money to your checking account.

Summary

Get cash whenever you can, accept personal checks from people you know and trust, accept credit and debit cards if you want to make more money overall. Paypal is a must if you plan to buy or sell on eBay.

Chapter 14
10 Quick Tips for Managing Expenses

Running a Business On a Budget

Managing expenses is important in a small business. Remember income is Revenue – COGs – Expenses. To increase income, we need to increase revenue, and/or lower expenses and COG's. COG's is pretty much out of our control except for purchasing in higher quantities or making purchases when suppliers have special pricing options.

Here are some expense managing tips that I have learned.

1. Don't buy things you don't need.
2. When considering a purchase, ask yourself if it is going to generate revenue, save time, or provide better quality. Remember, time is money.
3. Use coupons, take advantage of specials, and sign up for rewards programs. This especially works with office supplies. The place I have business cards periodically runs specials on printing. Their special is usually 1,000 cards for the price of 500. Fortunately, I am usually about out of business cards at the same time they run their special. In all my years in business, I've never paid full price for business cards.
4. Use as much free advertising as possible. Facebook, Twitter, Instagram, and Pinterest are free. Craigslist is another free online place to advertise items and services. E-mail is also a free way to get the word out about your business.

5. Take advantage of your supplier specials. One of my guitar case suppliers occasionally offers free shipping if you order over a certain dollar amount. This is significant because cases are bulky and expensive to ship.
6. Buy items in quantity if there are price breaks and it makes good business sense.
7. Recycle packaging. If you sell online, save boxes and packing materials you get from your suppliers and use them to ship to your customers.
8. Keep your utility costs low by adjusting the heat or air conditioning when you are closed. Having said this, you do need to keep in mind that guitars do not like extreme temperature changes. Use common sense with this one. Turn off computers and other devices at night.
9. If you need office furniture or store fixtures, buy them used. Craigslist is a good resource for this. Unfortunately, businesses are shutting down all the time, and they need to get rid of their furniture and fixtures. There are also businesses that specialize in selling used office furniture.
10. Bartering – I have run across lots of business owners who are willing to exchange products and services. We have bartered for signage, t-shirts, web design, and more.

Chapter 15
Debt, Borrowing Money, and Emergency Funds

The best advice I can give, is to keep your business and your personal life as debt free as possible. Debt costs money and it can be very expensive if not handled properly. Debt can even put you out of business if you're not careful.

I want you to read this book and get excited about making money in the guitar biz. However, please do not read this book and go out and rack up a credit card bill or huge debt to purchase tools, merchandise, advertising, rent on a building, etc.

This book is about making money in the guitar biz. As you have read it, you notice that I started out part time in my home with very little investment. It did grow quickly from there, but it was a controlled growth. I just kept reinvesting money back into the business. This has been an ongoing process and continues to grow year after year.

Throughout the course of my business, I have used a low interest line of credit through my bank. A line of credit is a pool of money you can borrow from instantly and repay quickly with no penalties. I also have taken out a couple of small business loans. One of them was when I moved to the new location and expanded my retail operation. I needed inventory to stock the showroom, so I took out a small business loan through my bank. The interest rate on that loan is much smaller than a typical credit card rate. In other words, if you need to borrow money, go see your banker.

There were times earlier in the course of my business where I racked up some credit card debt. Knowing what I do now, I will not let that happen again.

The following may seem like personal information or a plug, but I feel that in a book about making money it is relevant. In 2012, my wife and I took Dave Ramsey's Financial Peace University course. I highly recommend this to anyone. It is about personal finance, but it can be applied to business as well. It has been life-changing for us. It has altered how we manage money in our personal lives as well as the business. The class requires an investment of around $100. Notice I said investment, not cost. The knowledge and strategies gained from the class has generated a huge return on the $100 we spent. You can get more info at www.daveramsey.com.

When you own a small business, your paycheck is part of the profits generated by your business. You have to pay yourself what you need to live on, as well as have money left over to reinvest in the business. In order to sustain the business and succeed financially, you have to manage the business money as well as your personal money. They are tied together and one affects the other.

The Importance of an Emergency Fund for Your Small Business

Many Americans live paycheck to paycheck. Small business owners are usually no exception – especially startups. We pay ourselves the minimum amount to live on and invest as much as we can to grow the business.

However, unexpected business expenses may come up for which we are not prepared. What if you need an expensive repair or need to replace or buy a piece of equipment that is vital to your business? If you own a service oriented business and you are the main service provider, what happens if you get sick or have to take time off for other reasons? What happens if business suddenly slows down or stops?

An emergency fund can help your business cover those unexpected expenses. It is money set aside in an account that you don't touch unless it's absolutely necessary. Some people reach for the credit card for emergencies. However, debt costs money. The interest eats away at your profits. An emergency fund will help you avoid debt. It can cover for times when business slows down.

How much should your emergency fund be? If you don't have one, you can start small. How much money would you need if your business shut down for a week? That would be a good amount to start with and build on. Continue to build on the fund until you have a month's income if possible. Three months income would be even better.

How do you start an emergency fund? There are a couple ways to approach it. The first way is a lump sum. If you make a large sale, or have a month that exceeds what you normally do, put some of the excess money into the emergency fund. A simple savings account will work for this.

The second way is to set aside an amount each week and let the emergency fund build up. You can have it automatically transferred from your business checking account to a savings account on a weekly basis.

Determine what a good minimum balance should be in your emergency fund. Grow the emergency fund and replenish it as quickly as possible should you need to use it.

This strategy also works well for your personal money management as well. Get those emergency funds built up and maximize your profits by avoiding debt!

Chapter 16
Multiple Revenue Streams
Generate a River of Cash Flow

Some people believe in doing one thing and doing it well. Some businesses can survive with a limited product line and sell a lot of that product. What happens when the demand is reduced for the one thing you do well or someone else comes up with a product that is better or becomes more popular?

By having multiple revenue streams in your business, you have several "safety nets" in place. If one revenue stream slows down or dries up, there are others in place to keep the cash flow going.

I have several revenue streams flowing into my guitar business, but they are all related.

- Guitar Lessons – This is an example of where people are paying you for your time and knowledge, which is profitable as long as you have the time to devote to it. By giving private lessons you also generate store traffic. Lots of our retail sales come from our students. We've also added ukulele, mandolin, banjo and voice lessons to the mix which generates even more store traffic.
- Repair and Customizing – We repair and customize all types of fretted instruments and electronic music accessories. This is another example of being paid for our time. Parts sales for the repairs or upgrade parts and accessories also generate revenue.
- Online Sales – My online sales started when I stocked up on parts for the repair side of the business and suddenly I had lots of items sitting around not generating income. I started bundling parts together to make wiring kits for

popular models of electric guitars. We have expanded our online sales offerings and now have an eBay store and two other online stores. I call it making money while you sleep. Many online purchases are made late at night or in the wee morning hours. It's always nice to wake up in the morning with more money than when you went to bed. If you're in a retail business and not selling online, it may be something you want to consider.

- Group Classes – We currently offer three group classes and are looking into more. We do Guitar Building, Effects Pedal Building, and Tube Amplifier Building classes. These are good revenue generators as we are selling parts and time to multiple people simultaneously. If you know how to do something that you enjoy, chances are you can find other people who want to learn how to do it. For more info on this, see the chapter on Group Classes.

- Retail Sales – We started doing retail sales from the beginning, but have greatly expanded that part of the business since moving to a new location in a high traffic area. We added a showroom stocked with popular brands of guitars, ukuleles, banjos and mandolins. We chose brands that our local competitors did not carry and have various price points from quality beginner to professional level instruments.

- Performing – I am also a working musician which provides me with another revenue stream. While that is technically not part of the business, it does give me credibility with potential customers. It also gives me the opportunity to network. I have been approached at gigs and asked about guitar lessons. I have also had guitar players approach me and ask about the guitars I am playing, one of which is the demo model for the Guitar Building Class. See how this works? It gives me the opportunity to give a business card and my "elevator pitch" to someone who may not know about my business.

Those are the revenue streams that make up my business. As you can see, much of my revenue is generated by selling my time, which is very profitable.

I've found that certain parts of the revenue stream ebb and flow depending on the seasons. The retail portion picks up around the Christmas season, while the repairs slow down. Retail then slows the first quarter, but lessons pick up from all the people who got instruments for Christmas and want to learn to play them. Repairs pick up in the winter as well due to the dry air causing problems with acoustic guitars. Guitar customizing picks up in the spring when the working musicians are getting ready for the summer which is their busy time. My performance income increases over the summer as well, while lessons drop off due to vacations, etc. Lessons pick back up in the fall when school starts, and kids want to learn an instrument. Then the cycle repeats.

If you've discovered you have slow times during the year, be thinking about what you can do during those slow times. Also be thinking about ways to generate more store traffic if you're in retail. I know a guitar shop owner in Minnesota who also brews and sells coffee and energy drinks. While coffee and soft drinks are not related to guitars, it brings in store traffic of people who may not be interested in guitars...yet.

To summarize: Keep those revenue streams flowing into a river of cash flow. Think out of the box, and have plans for the slow times. Remember, cash flow can make or break a business.

Chapter 17

Boost Your Profits Using a Daily Business Plan

When you research starting a business, you will be told you need to write a business plan. This is true. You need to know if your business will generate enough profit to sustain and to pay yourself and any employees you need to hire. A business plan like this is a "big picture" strategy. However, a daily business plan can generate immediate results.

If you want to improve something, you need to measure it and focus on it. I have boosted my revenue and profits by using a simple daily business plan. I am in a service business where most of my profit is generated by selling my time. When you are selling your time, it's all about billable hours and revenue generating activities. There can be several distractions throughout the day. The phone rings, you get notifications from e-mail and social media. Customers walk in, who may or may not spend money on that particular visit. While you don't want to ignore walk in customers or phone calls, you should set aside a specific time to check and respond to social media and e-mail.

The daily business plan is very simple. Generate as much revenue and profit within a day that you can. Use a spreadsheet or generate a report from your accounting software to track your revenue, expenses, and profit on a daily basis.

How does this help? It will cause you to focus on increasing your revenue and watching expenses to boost profits. It helps with time management because it will cause you to spend more time on revenue generating activities.

Here are some time management strategies that help increase your billable time:

- Have your day planned prior to walking in the door. Look at your schedule the night before so when you walk in you can immediately start generating revenue.
- Have set times for checking e-mail and social media. Every morning I check e-mail, social media, and account balances from home before business hours. That way when I get into the shop, I can be productive on revenue generating activities right away. My next scheduled time to check these things is lunch time.
- Learn to ignore audio notifications from e-mail and social media throughout the day. You don't have to check them immediately. It doesn't seem like it would take long to check and respond to an e-mail or check a social media notification. Social media especially can be very distracting. Before you know it 30 minutes of potential billable time has slipped away with nothing to show for it.
- After you complete a revenue generating task and bill it out, glance at your e-mail and see if it is something that needs immediate attention. Can it wait while you move on to the next revenue generating activity?
- Have employees take care of tasks that take you away from revenue generating activities.
- If you don't have employees, run the numbers to see if you can justify hiring someone to take care of the tasks that take you away from billable hours.
- Train employees to do some of the tasks that generate higher revenues to increase your profits.

Focusing on the numbers on a daily basis and managing your time properly to get the most out of every day will help boost profits and make you more efficient. It will allow you to get work done in a timely manner. You will make more money and your customers will appreciate a faster turnaround time. It is a win-win strategy.

Chapter 18
Marketing and Advertising on A Budget

It doesn't matter how good you are at what you do if your potential customers don't know about your business. Fortunately, we are currently living in a time where social media allows you to market your business for free or very little money.

Develop An Online Presence

Almost everyone is online. If you are running or starting a business, having an online presence is a must. The cost of having several ways for people to find you is very low these days. Social media including Facebook, Twitter, Pinterest, Instagram, and YouTube are all FREE. You can get your message to thousands of people in an instant without spending a dime. Prior to social media, you had to spend thousands of dollars on print, radio, or TV advertising. Social media also lets you interact with your customers online, either privately or publicly.

Website

It's important to have a professional looking website. There are lots of templates available to design your own website. You just plug in the pictures and the text. WordPress is also a format that you can use. If you can afford it, paying someone with web design experience to create your website is a very good idea. However, make sure that you work with someone who will give you access to update your website to make changes when necessary. If you've got a new product that you want to announce, you want to be able to do that quickly. There are lots of books and resources available. Look at other websites of businesses similar to yours and see what they are doing. Make note of the things you like and don't like about theirs in order to get ideas.

Using Facebook to Grow Your Business

If you own a business or are starting one, Facebook is a very cost effective way to reach a lot of potential customers. In order to be effective, you need to use it properly. Here are some things I have learned through observation and my own experience. I am writing this assuming you are familiar with Facebook and the terminology. If you are not, set up a personal page and get familiar with posting photos, links, tagging, etc.

Do not use your personal page as your business page.

Keep your personal life personal, and your business page business. You can put items on your personal page that are related to your business, however. I have used Facebook to expand our customer base, sell items, sign people up for classes and keep our customers informed of new products or services we offer. I have also used it to get feedback and reviews from our customers.

Getting "Likes" for Your Business Page

In order for your message to get to people, they need to "Like" your page. You can start by inviting your personal friends to like your page. Also have links to your page on websites and anywhere you post online. You can also use QR codes that people can scan with their smartphones that will link them to your page. We have a sign in our store window with QR codes that link people to our Facebook, Twitter, e-mail list and Pinterest accounts.

Content and Timing

In order to be effective, your business Facebook page needs *quality* content and needs to be updated regularly. We typically update ours one to three times per day to keep our name in front of people. Determine when the best times are by trying different times of the day and see what responses you get. You want to post when you can reach the most potential customers. I have found the best times are early morning before people go to work, lunch time, and evening. You will get more response if you are posting pictures or videos. Another strategy to get interaction on Facebook is to post questions or surveys. Humor is also a nice touch. People like to laugh.

The 80/20 Rule

The 80/20 Rule means that only 20% of your Facebook posts are about marketing. The other 80% may be humor, pictures, tips, and video that will interest your followers. You can also use surveys to ask your customers their opinions. These surveys can be formal, or informal. An example may be posting a picture of a new model of guitar. It may be something unique to see what people think. Or find out which color of a certain model they would prefer.

Tagging

One strategy I use to get the same message out more than once is tagging photos at different times. I may post a photo on my business page in the morning along with comments. Later in the day or the next day, I'll tag the picture under the business name or my own personal name or both. Tagging the picture puts it back on peoples' newsfeed.

Also, whether I am personally in the picture or not, I tag myself. This goes to the newsfeed of my personal Facebook friends, who may or may not follow my business page. You never know when someone on your personal friend list may have a need for a product or service your business provides. I know I mentioned earlier that you should keep the personal and the business page separate and that is true to a point. People who know me personally know that guitar has been a big part of my life since childhood. I don't think my friends mind if I am tagged in a picture of new inventory arrivals at AM Guitar Works. Actually, many of my friends are musicians, so I know they don't mind.

I also think that people like to see others succeed. Many of my friends have been supportive and "cheerleaders" throughout this business venture whether they do business with me or not.

Having said that, I do keep my personal life off of my business page. Your customers don't need to know that you have a cold or that Uncle John and Aunt Susan are getting divorced. In my opinion some people just give too many details of their lives on Facebook. It's up to you what you post on your personal page, but keep your business page professional.

As a general rule, watch what you post on your personal Facebook page as well. If you own a small business, people associate you personally with the business. I have had people contact me interested in employment opportunities. I check out their FB pages and find their timelines littered with profanity, negativity, and pictures that are unbecoming of someone looking for a job. AM Guitar Works is a family friendly business. To my customers, I and my employees, *are* AM Guitar Works. A company is only as good as the people working there. Negativity, offensive language and bad behavior is not what I want reflected on my business.

Join Facebook Groups

There are usually groups on Facebook made up of people who have common interests. I am on a few groups with local musicians. These groups may be set up for people to advertise gear that they want to buy and sell. They may also be set up just for general discussions. If you are part of the group, you are able to offer advice, point them to your business, and get the word out. Just be careful not to overdo it. I have seen discussions get ugly on these groups or people complaining that professional retailers are posting too much. They look at it a discussion place and don't want a "hard sell".

In Summary

To sum it up, Facebook is a good way to get quick messages out to lots of people. I have used it to post items for sale, get rid of clearance items, sign up students, and keep my name in front of people. To see how I use Facebook to market my business, "Like" my page. www.facebook.com/amguitarworks

YouTube

YouTube is another free way to advertise. Producing a short video is pretty easy with today's technology. You can shoot the video with a digital camera, iPad, video camera, or even a smart phone.

We have started posting YouTube videos to demonstrate products and promotional material. A picture with text is one thing, but if you can see and hear a product in action with someone explaining it, that's huge. It used to be that you could only do this with an expensive 30 second TV spot. Now you can put several minutes of video on the internet with potentially millions of viewers. The trick is getting viewers to your YouTube channel.

This is another subject that has complete books written on this subject. There is also lots of information on the internet.

eBay
We discussed selling on eBay in detail earlier in this book. It is also another place people find you for things other than the items you have listed there. If you put your location in your listings, people who are nearby may find you there. People may also ask you for items you have that are not listed.

One day I had an eBay member ask me a question about a custom wiring kit I had listed for $25. I replied back to him with my contact information including my website. He got back with me and said not to ship the wiring kit as he would pick it up when he came up for my Guitar Building 101 class. He ended up spending over $900 with me because he ran across a small item I had listed.

Twitter, Pinterest and Instagram
These are other social media sites that you can use. Instagram is nice for posting pictures. Instagram can simultaneously post to your Facebook page and your Twitter account. We do "Shop Shots" where we take a picture of a repair in progress or

completed and post it to Instagram. It automatically goes to our Facebook and Twitter accounts as well.

E-mail

Start collecting e-mail addresses from your customers and potential customers. Send out e-mail on a regular basis. I do not recommend sending daily e-mails, but one to four times per month is good. It is more effective to send more e-mails with a little information than one long e-mail with tons of info.

We use Mail Chimp to put together professional looking e-mails. You can easily add photos and edit text. It will also generate reports so you can see who opened your e-mail, who clicked on links, etc.

Craigslist

Craigslist is a great place to advertise products and services. Many of our new customers find us through our ads there. The best thing about it is that it's FREE!

We used to sporadically post items on Craigslist and when we focused on it we would get more walk-in traffic. We decided we should not be sporadic, but have a schedule that we followed. If you have a plan on paper, it's easy to execute rather than be sporadic.

We put every instrument and amplifier we have in inventory on an Excel spreadsheet. We have columns for Brand, Model, Serial number, and Description. We also have columns to enter the dates we posted the item on Craigslist, Facebook, Twitter, and Instagram. In order to "mix it up" I first sorted the spreadsheet by Brand and Model. Then I edited the spreadsheet so that the brands were in a rotation. That way people see the variety of items that we carry.

Our goal is to list an item on Craigslist every day. Besides the "featured item" in the listing, we have a couple paragraphs describing what products and services we offer. We also post pictures of our showroom in addition to photos of the featured item.

Musicians are always looking at Craigslist. If you want new customers, you have to go where they are looking.

Other Online Marketing Opportunities

There are several ways you can get your name out. You can comment on guitar related posts on Facebook. You can do reviews on websites. One of my main luthier tool suppliers, Stewart MacDonald, lets you review products on their website. I review their products when I buy them. My signature is "Alan Morrison – AM Guitar Works Davenport, IA". Let's say someone in my area is thinking of doing their own repair on a guitar and they need this tool. They may figure out that it would be better if they brought it to a professional rather than spending money on the item.

Networking

I network everywhere I go. My car has logos on the doors and my web address on the back window. The van my wife drives also has the website on the back as well. It is very inexpensive to get this done and it has generated a lot of business. One of my best customers found me because he saw one of our vehicles.

I have shirts and a jacket embroidered with my business name and logo. My customer base has grown because people saw me standing in line at the bank or at a convenience store. I signed up a new student recently because I went to a health screening and the nurse commented on my shirt.

Always be ready with your "elevator pitch". This is a summary about your business that you could give in an elevator ride.

T-Shirts

T-Shirts are another way to advertise. We charge a $10 registration fee for new guitar students. We give them a free t-shirt when they register. The registration fee covers the cost of the shirt. That way we have people wearing our name to school, the mall, and other places.

Imprinted Guitar Picks

What better way to advertise to guitar players than with picks imprinted with your logo and business name. The owner of Legend Picks is here in the Quad Cities. He has made picks for several major artists. He is also one of my customers. You can see his work at www.legendpicks.com

Speaking Engagements

I have been asked to speak in front of entrepreneur and small business classes. I've also been asked to come in as the "expert" at the preschool where my wife teaches when they were studying guitars or ukuleles.

Getting in front of people telling my story has paid off. I spoke to a group of college students who were in an entrepreneurial class. After the speech, one of the students asked if he could see my shop, so I had him follow me there. He spent $80 on parts that day. A few weeks later, the professor came in and spent over $800 on a new guitar, an amp and accessories.

Speaking at a pre-school has generated sales of ukuleles and lessons.

Don't be afraid to put yourself out there. Every situation is an opportunity to grow your business.

Newspaper Articles
If you have the opportunity, get your business in the newspaper. Contact a reporter who does articles for the business section of your local paper. Get creative and do something newsworthy. We had an article written in July of 2010 in the *Quad City Times*. It launched my business to a new level. Lots of people found out about me very quickly. It didn't hurt that it was a full page on the front cover of the Business section on Sunday, July 4. Since they have an online newspaper as well, that added to our online presence and the search engines would find it.

We have also had an article in the *Rock Island Argus* which generated more business.

I was also interviewed as an expert a few years ago for a newspaper article on the increased popularity of the ukulele. Becoming known as an expert gives you more opportunities for exposure.

Word of Mouth – The Best Free Advertising!
I used to have a boss that would say, "The reward for good work is more work." I didn't always care for this statement, but when

you are in business and your income depends on how much work you do, it rings true.

Most of the growth of my business has come from referrals from friends, relatives, and satisfied customers. In the guitar business, this can be huge. Musicians tend to hang out together, talk in person, and online. If you provide a great experience for one person, they will refer you to their friends. This is one of the things I keep in mind whenever working on a customer's instrument. If they are happy with the work I do on this guitar, they will bring me more to repair as well as send their friends.

Chapter 19
Selling Guitars 101

You've marketed your business and you are driving traffic to your shop. That's great, but it does you no good until people buy products or services from you. In this chapter, I will discuss some selling basics, mostly as they relate to a retail guitar shop. However, these apply to all aspects of your business. If you're giving lessons or doing repairs, you need to know how to sell your services.

There are thousands of books dedicated to sales techniques and I highly recommend you don't make this chapter the only thing you read on the subject. *Secrets of Closing the Sale* by Zig Ziglar was a big influence on me when I read it in the early '80's. I have read it again many times since then. A lot of my sales strategies can be traced back to that book.

Selling Is Communication
Selling is a communication process. We communicate through the words we speak, the tone we use, our appearance and our body language.

Before we even open our mouth to speak, we have communicated to the customer. Are you dressed properly for where you work? The guitar biz is pretty casual, so you don't need to wear a suit and tie, of course. I usually wear a polo or button down shirt with our company logo embroidered on it. I stay away from t-shirts. They're just too casual for meeting with customers. In the winter I wear jeans. In the summer, I wear khaki shorts. I spend long hours repairing guitars, working the showroom, and giving lessons. I need to be comfortable, but not disheveled.

Body Language
Body language is also important. Keep a smile on your face. When talking to customers avoid crossing your arms. It makes you look defensive. Avoid looking at your watch or your phone to check the time. It gives the appearance that you don't have time for the customer. Look customers in the eye, but don't stare them down.

Listening Skills
A huge part of the communication process is listening. You've heard the adage we are given one mouth and two ears, so focus twice as much on listening as you do speaking.

What are we listening for? We want to find out what the customer's needs or concerns are. We also want to listen for buying signals. Buying signals are communicated through body language and voice. A buying signal is something the customer says or does that tells you there is an opportunity for a sale to be made.

Steps in the Sales Process
The outline below shows the steps in a basic sales process. This applies to selling any product, but we are going to specifically discuss guitar sales in detail.

1. Know your product
2. Greet with a good first impression

3. Qualify the customer – what are they looking for and what are the requirements to get the deal? How much are they planning to spend?
4. Discuss possibilities then features and benefits of each of the options. Narrow down the choices.
5. Close the sale.

Know Your Product
This is preparation before you ever talk to potential customers. If you're selling guitars, know the features such as wood types, electronics and hardware. When it comes to selling acoustic guitars, knowing how the different types of wood relate to the tone of the guitar is important. You may be dealing with people who have no idea what they are looking for, or you may be selling to someone who is knowledgeable and has done their research. You want to know at least as much as they do. People will trust you more if you know your products inside and out.

Greeting the Customer
The sales process begins from the time the potential customer walks in the door. When a customer walks in, shake their hand, greet them with a smile, and ask how you can help them today. If you haven't met, introduce yourself. "Hello, how can I help you today?" Listen for their response, then reply. "I'm (insert your name here). I am the owner," (if that's the case). Then respond to their answer to your "How can I help you?" question. This helps establish an instant rapport and helps you find out why they came in.

Qualify the Customer

This is where you ask probing questions to find out more details on what the customer is wanting. If they come in and tell you they are looking for a new guitar, you need to find out if they need electric or acoustic. If it's an acoustic guitar, do they need electric capabilities? What do they plan on spending? Are they purchasing it for themselves or is it a gift? I also make conversation with the customer. This helps establish trust.

Here's a scenario that you might see in a guitar shop. The potential customer is standing in your showroom, arms folded. They are "just looking". This is not a buying signal. Get them to open up a little. Grab a guitar you think they might have their eye on and ask if they would like to play it. You might say something like, "This is our most popular model. Would you like to give it a try?" At this point, they can reply with a yes or a no. If no is the answer, chances are they are not interested in making a purchase at this time. If yes is the answer, you are making headway and you continue with the selling process.

Here is another scenario. Someone comes in and says they are looking for a guitar. You've already got a buying signal, so now is the time to start asking open ended questions. These are questions that cannot be answered with a simple one word answer, such as yes, no or maybe. These are the questions that will get you the information you need in order to get them the guitar they need. Remember the five W's? Who, what, when, where and why?

Who - Who are they? Are they an adult or young person? Are they a beginner or have they been playing awhile? Do they play for their own enjoyment or are they a working musician? Are they buying this as a gift? If it's a gift, then you have to probe to answer the above questions about who the recipient is.

What - What are they looking for? Electric, acoustic, or acoustic/electric? What is their price range? What kind of music do they play?

When– When do they need it? Would they like to take it home today? "If I special order the red one, would you be able to pick it up next week?"

Where– Where will they be playing their guitar? Will they be playing at school, church, coffee shops, bar gigs, arenas, or at home? Tip: If they are playing anywhere besides home, be sure to recommend a hardshell case once you've closed the deal. I usually wait until after they've committed to buying the guitar before mentioning the extras.

Why– Why do they need a new guitar? Are they just getting started? Have they outgrown their beginner model? Are they looking for something with more features? Are they looking for something flashy or something subdued? The Christmas after my son got his Music Therapy degree I let him choose any guitar he wanted from my showroom. We had some very decorative, pretty guitars. He chose one that was just a gloss finish over a spruce top with a wood inlay rosette. As a Music Therapist, he didn't want to have something that was too distracting. This was something I would have never thought of.

You can find out all of this information by asking simple, probing questions. If they are trying guitars and playing them, don't interrupt their playing. Ask questions if they pause or

157

make a comment. You don't want to make them feel like you're interrogating them. Asking the questions helps you build a rapport with them. I also make sure I complement their playing. They may give you some of the information you need in conversation, without you having to ask questions. Be sure to listen to them.

Discussing Options, Features, and Benefits
Once you know what the customer is looking for and their price range, you can offer them some options. I usually show them something in their price range and try to find what best meets their needs. Then I show them something that is a little higher than the price range they mentioned. Many times a customer is willing to spend a little more than they quoted if you sell them on the value of the higher priced model. A good example might be someone who is looking for an acoustic guitar. Ask them if they want a straight acoustic or an acoustic/electric guitar. If they're not sure, I encourage them to get one with built-in electronics. Explain that electronics can be installed on an acoustic guitar later, but in the long run it's more expensive than purchasing one with factory installed electronics. Try to get customers to think long term.

When pointing out features, make sure you explain how those features will benefit the customer. Explain how a solid top is preferable vs. a laminated top acoustic guitar. For electric guitars, you can talk about pickups, hardware, electronics and other features. If you are selling to someone who is a "shredder" and wants to do whammy bar "dive bombs", then something with a locking tremolo would best fit their needs.

Closing the Sale

The most important step in the process is closing the sale. You don't get any money until that happens. There are several closing strategies, but the main thing in all of them is that you ask for the sale, multiple times if necessary. One mistake many amateur salespeople do is to forget to ask for the sale. They might be good at knowing their products and demoing guitars, but if you don't give the customer a chance to say yes, the customer might walk out without making a purchase.

If you've ever been in a sales career, you've heard ABC – Always Be Closing. When someone is in the showroom looking at instruments, I ask, "Is today new guitar day?" This is a closed ended question that can be answered with a "yes", "no" or "maybe". Their answer tells you right away what your chances are of making a sale. Don't rule out your chances even if they say "no" at this point, though. Once you establish a rapport, and they play some instruments, they may find that it is indeed "new guitar day".

"The Choice" Close

Once you have discussed features and benefits of the different models that suit their needs, it's time to give them a choice. "Would you like to take home the guitar with the spruce top or the one with the cedar top?" "Do you want the red one or the blue one?"

"My Expert Opinion" Close

Some people have a hard time making decisions. This is where you come in with your expert opinion. This close will usually be used when helping a customer who is new to buying guitars or is buying a gift. You could say, "It's a tough decision, but I've purchased many guitars over the years and have been in the business a long time. If you want my professional opinion, I would go with this one." Then tell them the reasons why. After explaining the reasons, then ask, "Does that sound good to you?"

The "Buy Both" Close
This is another one I use when people are undecided between two instruments. "I always tell people when they can't decide, they should buy both!" Then we laugh a little. It lightens the mood and takes the pressure off. Then say, "Seriously, which one is going to best fit your needs now and long term?" You can also use the "expert opinion" close above as a follow up to this close. Recently I used this close, and to my surprise, the customer DID buy both guitars!

The "Go Big or Go Home" Close
This is one my daughter used and shared with me. I have since used it as well. We had a customer in the store and he was trying some of our nicer guitars. He had a price range in mind, but was really drawn to one that was higher priced. He seemed willing to spend more money, though. Brianna told him if he bought the lower priced guitar, he would still want the higher priced one and end up coming back to get it anyway. Then she said, "I always say 'Go big or go home, right?'" He ended up purchasing the more expensive acoustic/electric guitar, a hardshell case, an amplifier and a cable.

The "Fear of Loss" Close
This is one that has stuck with me ever since I read *Secrets of Closing the Sale*. "The fear of loss is greater than the desire for gain." This is true of the human psyche. If we see something we

think we want, we fear missing out on it more than we actually want or need the item.

This can be used if you have promotions or sales. "If you want this guitar, now is the time to buy it. You don't want to miss out on the special pricing that ends this month."

"This is a beautiful guitar, but for some reason the manufacturer has discontinued this color. If you like it, I would buy it now because there aren't going to be any more once this one's gone." Of course, make sure you are telling the truth here. I have run across this situation, though and used it to close sales.

The "Fear of Loss" close works especially well with used items. "We've gone through this guitar and made sure it plays and sounds great. At this price, it's not going to be here long. I'd recommend if you want it, to buy it right away before someone else snatches it up."

Don't Forget the Extras!
Once you've closed the deal on the guitar, now it's time to add the extras. "Would you prefer a gig bag or a hardshell case? If you are planning to take the guitar out of the house quite a bit, a hardshell case will better protect your investment."

The extras are items that help increase your profits and also provide the customer with the necessary things they need so they don't have to make another trip to your shop (or heaven forbid another shop or buying online from someone other than you).

161

Bundling Accessories

A good suggestion is putting together accessory bundles. I recommend four choices. You can call them bronze, silver, gold and platinum as an example. You can have electric guitar packages and acoustic guitar packages.

The Bronze package can be the bare minimum you need when you get a new guitar. Include picks, a nylon strap and a gig bag. Some people may already own accessories in the other packages, so all they need is the minimum.

The Platinum package will be the best of the best. It may include a deluxe hardshell case, picks, leather strap, capo, electronic tuner, fingerboard conditioner, polish and cloth, humidifier, etc.

The Silver and Gold packages will be somewhere in between the Bronze and the Platinum. You will most likely sell more Silver and Gold packages than the other two.

If you have four options, people will usually pick one of the middle two, the silver or gold. A few will settle for the bronze package. Some people will spare no expense and pick the platinum package.

We use this mostly around Christmas time when many guitars are being purchased. The bundles can be saved as Memorized Receipts in Quickbooks, the accounting software we use. This saves time at checkout. It also makes it easier when selling because you only have to sell one thing as opposed to six or seven things.

Have your packages with the items included listed on a piece of paper in a sheet protector and keep it handy. Once you have closed the sale on the guitar, get out the sheet and sell them the appropriate accessory package for their needs.

Sales Promotions
We usually offer some sort of monthly promotion at our shop. We base it on what our sales needs are at the time.

For example, if our electric guitars haven't been moving as fast as we'd like, we run a sale. Sometimes we offer a discount price or we offer to throw in a FREE gig bag with any purchase of an electric guitar. We can be brand or model specific. We may not want all our guitars to be sale priced.

If repairs have been slow, we offer a "buy one set of strings and get the second one free when you get your guitar set up" sale.

Another promotion we've offered to boost sales is "Free Strings for a Year" when you purchase a new guitar. We do this promotion a couple times a year, especially at Christmas.

We give the customer a punch card with January through December on it. We write which month the free strings start. They have to come in every month to pick up a set of free strings. We tell them if they miss a month, they miss out on that set of strings. This keeps them coming to the store twelve times a year to get their strings. Many times they look around to see what's new, or bring a friend in the shop with them. They also may purchase additional items when they pick up their strings.

The main thing when selling guitars is to be creative. Think of your own promotions and make them unique.

A Typical Selling Scenario

Here is a typical scenario you might see at my store. Imagine yourself as the customer. For right now, your name is going to be Pat and you are thinking it would be nice to have a new acoustic guitar. Are you ready?

You walk in the front door of my store. You hear some nice guitar music playing over the speakers. I put down the guitar I'm working on and come and greet you with a smile and a handshake.

Me: "Hi, my name is Alan. I'm the owner here. What can I help you with today?"

You: "Hi Alan, I'm Pat. I'm looking for an acoustic guitar."

Me: "Ok. Is today new guitar day?"

You: "Possibly. Right now I'm just looking."

Me: "Sure, no problem, Pat. Let's take a look at some. We'll figure out what best fits your needs and your price range". We walk into the showroom. "Will you be using this guitar to play at home, or will you be taking it out and playing in public?"

You: "For right now, just at home. Eventually I'd like to get to the point where I could play at church or some open mic nights."

Me: "Great! I would definitely recommend that you go with an acoustic/electric guitar then. Typically the price difference between similar models with and without electronics is only $50. It's much more than that to have electronics installed at a later date. What price range did you have in mind?"

You: "I don't want to spend a lot of money, but I want something nice. Can I get a decent one for around $250?"

Me: "Sure. Let me show you this Festival Series guitar. It's right in your price range. I have one with a plain top for $249 and one with a flamed maple top for $279. The main difference is the appearance. The plain top is a little more subdued looking. The flamed maple top is a little more elegant for $30 more. Which one would you like to try first?"

You: "Let me try the flamed maple top one."

Me: "Sure. It's a gorgeous guitar. It's a smaller body guitar called a mini jumbo. These became popular in the MTV Unplugged days if you're familiar with that."

I take the guitar down and let you play it awhile.

Me: "What do you think, Pat?"

You: "It's ok I guess, but I'm not sure it's the one."

Me: "Well let me show you our top selling model. This is the Heritage Series. It's a little more money, but it's got some nice features.

You notice it's a dreadnaught size guitar, which is a bigger body than the Festival Series. The other difference is that this guitar has a solid spruce top as opposed to the laminated top of the Festival series. A solid top is more desirable because the top of the guitar is where the sound comes from. A laminated top is a thin, pretty piece of wood laminated or glued over a cheaper piece of wood."

Before I hand the guitar to you I strum an E chord on it. When you hand me the lower priced guitar, I strum an E chord on it.

Me: "Can you hear the difference?"

You: "Oh, yes. There's definitely a difference in sound. The Heritage series has a fuller sound."

Me: "That's because of the solid top, the larger body size and the mahogany back and sides."

You play the guitar for awhile and pause to look the guitar over.

Me: "How do you like it, Pat? Does it play well for you?"

You: "Yes, it plays great!"

Me: "Thank you. We do setups on all the guitars before they go in the showroom. These guitars are manufactured overseas, warehoused in Mississippi, and then shipped to our store here in Iowa. As you can imagine, they go through some humidity and temperature changes before they arrive here. We check and adjust the neck relief, nut slot depths and bridge saddle height to make them play their best. That's how we compete with the big box stores and the online sellers. If you bought this guitar online and brought it to me for a setup I would charge you a minimum of $60 to set it up."

You: "It sounds like you really care about taking care of your customers."

Me: "Yes. I come from a repair and guitar teaching background. The guitar teacher in me knows what it's like to see a student struggle trying to learn on a guitar that doesn't play well. The repairman part of me knows I can make that guitar play better than when it came out of the box. That guitar looks good on you, by the way. This one in particular has a beautiful wood grain. Would you like to hear it plugged in?"

You: "Sure."

Me: "Ok. I'll plug you into this Fishman Loudbox Mini. It's a great acoustic amp with lots of features. You should consider one of these when you're ready to amplify your guitar... Or you can take it home today if you'd like."

You: "No, I'm not ready for the amp yet. I'll get the guitar first and practice a little more."

You play the guitar a little and I show you some of the amps features. I know I'm probably not going to sell you an amp today, but I am planting the seed for a future sale.

You: "This guitar sounds really good plugged in or unplugged."

Me: "Yes. I think if you're going to be mostly playing at home, you will like the sound of this guitar better than the smaller bodied ones. Shall we get this one ready for you?"

You: "I really like it, but it's a little bit more than I wanted to spend."

Me: "I understand. I've learned the hard way several times that it's best to spend a little more now and get what suits your needs. If all you consider is price, you get the lower priced one and spend a few months wishing you would have got the one that suits your needs. Then you come back and buy the higher priced one eventually. So you could spend $250 today, then in six months or a year spend $330 making a total of $580 to get what you could have paid $330 for in the first place."

You: "Yes, that makes sense."

Me: "The decision is up to you, but in my expert opinion I would recommend this one. So would you like the Heritage Series or the smaller Festival Series?"

You: "I'm going to take the Heritage Series. It will be a better deal long term."

Me: "Excellent choice. Now we should talk about a few extras to go with your guitar. We make it easy for you, though. We have four different accessory packages for you to choose from. Let's take a look at those."

Here the sales process starts over with the accessory packages, but this should be quick.

Once you've decided on the package and have checked out, I continue the conversation.

Me: "Thank you for doing business with us. Is it ok if we take a picture of you with your new guitar? Are you ok if we post the picture on our Facebook page?"

You: "Sure. That would be ok."

We take a picture of you smiling with your new guitar.

Me: "Thanks for choosing AM Guitar Works. Let us know if there's anything else we can do for you. Be sure to recommend us to your musician friends as well."

I wanted you to picture yourself as the customer in this scenario because I wanted you to think about how you would feel in this situation. Nobody likes a hard sell. You can see I was very casual and not pushy. I was more concerned about seeing you get what best suited your needs. This particular style best matches my personality and the atmosphere of my store. You will find what works best for you. Now, let's analyze what took place here.

Scenario Replay with Commentary
Did you catch the sales techniques I used here? Let's replay the scenario, this time with commentary.The comments are in ***bold italics***.

You walk in the front door of my store. You hear some cool guitar music playing. ***We use Pandora internet radio in the***

shop with a wide variety of music playing. We hear everything from classic rock to classical to bluegrass music. It's all guitar oriented which makes for a good music store atmosphere.
I put down the guitar I'm working on and come and greet you with a smile and a handshake. *Immediately dropping what I am doing shows that right now you are the most important person here. By greeting you with a smile and a handshake I am establishing a rapport with you and gaining your trust.*

Me: "Hi, my name is Alan. I'm the owner here. *Where else do you get to talk to the owner? Only use this if you ARE the owner, of course.*
What can I help you with today?" *This is an open ended question to find out why the customer is here.*

You: "Hi Alan, I'm Pat. I'm looking for an acoustic guitar." *Make sure you catch their name. You need to use it during your presentation.*

Me: "Ok. Is today new guitar day?" *This is a closed ended question. I'm finding out how hard I'll have to work to get this sale.*

You: "Possibly. Right now I'm just looking." *A buying signal! "Possibly" is better than "no".*

Me: "Sure, no problem. Let's take a look at some. We'll figure out what best fits your needs and your price range". We walk into the showroom. "Will you be using this guitar to play at home, or will you be taking it out and playing in public?" *Probing to find out the customer's needs.*

170

You: "For right now, just at home. Eventually I'd like to get to the point where I could play at church or some open mic nights."

Me: "Great! I would definitely recommend that you go with an acoustic/electric guitar then. Typically the price difference between similar models with and without electronics is only $50. It's much more than that to have electronics installed at a later date. What price range did you have in mind?" *I am starting to sell the value of a guitar with electronics and getting the customer to think long term.*

You: "I don't want to spend a lot of money, but I want something nice. Can I get a decent one for around $250?"

Me: "Sure, Pat."*People like to hear their names. I am also answering his question with a positive statement. We keep guitars in every price range so we can have something for everyone. Many times we use the lower priced ones to sell the value of higher priced instruments.* "Let me show you this Festival Series guitar. It's right in your price range. I have one with a laminated spruce top for $249 and one with a flamed maple top for $279. The main difference is the appearance. The plain top is a little more subdued looking. The flamed maple top is a little more elegant for $30 more. Which one would you like to try first?"

You: "Let me try the flamed maple top one." *Now I know you're willing to consider spending more than the $250 you originally quoted. Sometimes people will quote less than they are willing to spend in order to deal on price.*

171

Me: "Sure. It's a gorgeous guitar. It's a smaller body guitar called a mini jumbo. These became popular in the MTV Unplugged days if you're familiar with that."

I take the guitar down and let you play it awhile.

Me: "What do you think?" *This is an open ended question to see what you're thinking.*

You: "It's ok, I guess, but I'm not sure it's the one." *I know to move on now. If it's not the one, I'm not going to push you into buying it.*

Me: "Well let me show you our top selling model. This is the Heritage Series. It's a little more money, but it's got some nice features." *By saying "our top selling model", I am telling the customer many people have made the decision to buy this one. They can't all be wrong.*

What I do next is start selling the benefits and value of the more expensive guitar.

"You notice it's a dreadnaught size guitar, which is a bigger body than the Festival Series. The other difference is that this guitar has a solid spruce top as opposed to the laminated top of the Festival series. A solid top is more desirable because the top of the guitar is where the sound comes from. A laminated top is a thin, pretty piece of wood laminated or glued over a cheaper piece of wood." *Here's where knowing your product features and benefits comes in handy.*

Before I hand the guitar to you, I strum an E chord on it. When you hand me the lower priced guitar, I strum an E chord on it.

Me: "Can you hear the difference in tone?" *A closed ended question that I'm sure will be answered with a "Yes". I am moving the conversation in a positive direction.*

You: "Oh, yes. There's definitely a difference in sound. The Heritage series has a fuller sound."

Me: "That's because of the solid top, the larger body size and the mahogany back and sides." *Again, know your product!*

You play the guitar for awhile and pause to look the guitar over.

Me: "How do you like it? Does it play well for you?" *An open ended question followed by a closed ended question that I know will most likely be a "yes".*

You: "Yes, it plays great!" *Buying signal!*

Me: "Thank you. We do setups on all the guitars before they go in the showroom. These guitars are manufactured overseas, warehoused in Mississippi, and then shipped to our store here in Iowa. As you can imagine they go through some humidity and temperature changes before they arrive here. We check and adjust the neck relief, nut slot depths and bridge saddle height to make them play their best. That's how we compete with the big box stores and the online sellers. If you bought this guitar online and brought it to me for a setup I would charge you a minimum of $60 to set it up." *The customer sounds sold on the guitar. Now I have to sell them on buying from me as opposed to ordering online or going elsewhere to shop around. This also shows we know our product inside and out.*

You: "It sounds like you really care about taking care of your customers." *Buying signal!*

Me: "Yes. I come from a repair and guitar teaching background. The guitar teacher in me knows what it's like to see a student struggle trying to learn on a guitar that doesn't play well. The repairman part of me knows I can make that guitar play better than when it came out of the box. That guitar looks good on you, by the way." *This is a great line to make the customer feel good about the guitar.* "This one in particular has a beautiful wood grain." *This is just a subtle bit of the "fear of loss" close. Mentioning how nice the wood grain is on this particular guitar states that the next one to come in might not be as nice.* Would you like to hear it plugged in?" *This is a closed ended question with a likely "yes" answer to keep the conversation going positive.*

You: "Sure." *Buying signal!*

Me: "Ok. I'll plug you into this Fishman Loudbox Mini. It's a great acoustic amp with lots of features. You should consider one of these when you're ready to amplify your guitar... Or you can take it home today if you'd like." *From our conversation, I am pretty sure I'm not going to sell you an amp today, but I am planting the seed for a future sale. I want you to think long term.*

You: "No, I'm not ready for the amp yet. I'll get the guitar first and practice a little more." *Buying signal!*

You play the guitar a little and I show you some of the amps features.

You: "This guitar sounds really good plugged in or unplugged." *Buying signal!*

Me: "Yes. I think if you're going to be mostly playing at home, you will like the sound of this guitar better than the smaller bodied ones. Shall we get this one ready for you?" *I just asked you for a sale.*

You: "I really like it, but it's a little bit more than I wanted to spend." *Here's a subtle objection from the customer, but it is easily overcome. Don't give up!*

Me: "I understand. I've learned the hard way several times that it's best to spend a little more now and get what suits your needs. If all you consider is price, you can get the lower priced one today and spend a few months wishing you would have got the one that suits your needs. Then you come back and buy the higher priced one eventually. So you could spend $250 today, then six months or a year later, spend $330 making a total of $580 to get what you really wanted. When you do the math it makes more sense to spend $330 today, correct?" *You can't argue with math. Many people have been in this situation and they will recall it.*

You: "Yes, that makes sense." *Buying signal!*

Me: "The decision is up to you, but in my expert opinion I would recommend this one. So would you like the Heritage Series or the smaller Festival Series?" *I just threw a one-two punch with the "Expert Opinion" close followed by the "Choice" close.*

You: "I'm going to take the Heritage Series. It will be a better deal long term." *Sold! We're not done yet, though. It's time to add some accessories.*

Me: "Excellent choice!" *Reassure the customer they made the right decision.* "Now we should talk about a few extras to go with your guitar. We make it easy for you, though. We have four different accessory packages for you to choose from. Let's take a look at those."

Here the sales process starts over with the accessory packages, but this should be quick.

Once you've decided on the package and have checked out, I continue the conversation.

Me: "Thank you for doing business with us. Is it ok if we take a picture of you with your new guitar? Are you ok if we post the picture on our Facebook page?" *Most people are ok with this. Some are not, and we respect that. If the person getting a new guitar is a child, we always get the parent's permission.*

You: "Sure. That would be ok."

We keep an iPad or digital camera handy so we can take people's pictures with guitars they buy from us. With their permission, we put them on our Facebook page. We also offer to email them a picture so they can post it on their page as well.

Several of our customers have made these their Facebook profile pictures. These pictures are great marketing tools.

Me: "Thanks for choosing AM Guitar Works. Let us know if there's anything else we can do for you. Be sure to recommend us to your musician friends as well." *Here I am thanking you for your business. I am also subtly asking for future business from you. I am also asking for referrals.*

Summary
Selling guitars and related items is not difficult if you know your product and follow the steps. Sales were difficult for me at first, but the more I do, the easier it gets. The key to being great at sales is to find out what the customer's needs and wants are. Continue learning new techniques by reading books and online articles. Always be closing and always be learning.

Chapter 20
Customer Service

Customer service is a HUGE factor in the survival and growth of a small business. If you provide excellent customer service, not only will you get repeat business, but people will refer others to you via word of mouth and social media. Provide poor customer service and those same things can work against you. Before Facebook and Twitter, a poor customer service experience may have been told to 10 people. In this new social media era, a bad experience can and will be relayed to a person's hundreds or thousands of "friends" or "followers". There is little room for error these days.

How would you define excellent customer service? You've heard the phrase "You never get a second chance at a first impression." When a customer walks into my business they are greeted by someone with a smile, a handshake and an introduction. If I am greeting them, I introduce myself as the owner of the business. The owner won't be greeting them at the big box store if they are greeted at all.

Since I own a small guitar shop, I am usually able to spend time conversing with the customer. I ask questions to find out what their interests are and what they are looking for. I tell them about all the products and services we offer and how we differentiate ourselves from the competition. I thank them for stopping by whether they made a purchase or not. I want the customer to leave feeling like AM Guitar Works is a good, trustworthy place to do business. People may not remember your name, but they will always remember how you made them feel.

In a perfect world, nothing would ever go wrong and customers would never have a complaint or issue with our product or service. However, we know that issues are going to arise. It is how you handle the issue or complaint that will determine whether that customer gives you more business or not. When a complaint or issue occurs, it is an opportunity to rise to the occasion and make your business look good. I did customer service training seminars in my previous career. We taught the LAFN strategy and it worked well. No, we don't laugh at our customers. It was an acronym that was easy to remember.

- Listen
- Apologize
- Fix the problem
- Notify a Supervisor (if applicable)

Listening skills are important. Let the customer speak. Don't interrupt. If they are upset, let them vent. If they are raising their voice, speak calmly when you talk to them. Raising your voice only escalates the situation. Start moving the conversation in a positive direction. Ask questions that you know will be answered with a "Yes". Use the "Language of Yes" to tell them what you CAN do for them.

Apologize – An apology is not an admission of guilt or wrong doing. The customer is obviously not happy, so you need to apologize for the situation. If it was something you or your company did wrong, admit it and tell the customer steps that will be taken so that it doesn't happen again.

Fix the problem – The quicker you address the issue, the better. One of my supervisors in a previous career used a shotgun analogy. He said putting off addressing a negative situation just gives them time to load the other barrel. If it is something that can't be resolved on the spot or is going to take awhile to resolve, stay in touch with the customer to keep them up to date.

If you're an employee, notify your supervisor if applicable. In any size business a manager or owner should be notified if there is a customer issue. There is nothing worse for an owner or manager than being "blind-sided" by a customer issue that an employee should have notified them of. If you're the supervisor or owner, this gives you an opportunity to follow up with the customer.

Finally as a consumer, study the customer service of the places you do business with. Visit your competitors or similar business. What kind of feeling do you get about their business? What did they do right? Did they do anything that impressed you? Did they seem indifferent? Were you treated poorly? Make sure you emulate their positive traits and avoid the negative traits in your business. Provide above and beyond customer service and you will be successful.

Chapter 21
Competition

When I launched my business, the timing couldn't have been better. The guy who was doing lots of guitar repair work had just moved away. I saw this as an opportunity to fill a need, so I ramped up my business quickly by launching a website and Facebook page. I visited local music stores and dropped off business cards and started getting work from a lesson studio and a large guitar store.

Other people who did guitar work also saw the need and were starting to advertise. The large guitar store started doing repairs in house. At first, this bothered and concerned me because I wanted my business to be THE place to go. As it turns out, there is plenty of work to go around and by this time my customer base was built up enough to sustain and grow the business.

I had an epiphany and have come to think of competition based on this philosophy. "Don't worry about the competition. Let them worry about me." That may sound overly confident or braggadocious, but allow me to explain. It is what I tell myself to keep my business growing and moving forward. You can spend time and energy worrying about your competitors, or you can focus on moving forward and improving your business. Hopefully they are doing the same.

Competition is healthy because it means everyone has to be on top of their game to succeed. If there was only one place to go and their work was sub-par, people would still go there because it was their only choice. If there are several places competing for the same customer base, the ones who are best at running their businesses will have the most success, and they deserve it. What competition does is improve the overall quality available to the customers in your area.

Dare To Be Different

My shop may not be the biggest one in town, but I believe it is unique in several ways when compared to my competitors. The group classes, for example, are something AM Guitar Works does that no one else around does. My repair shop and lesson studio are in the front windows instead of hidden away in the back of the store. We do more in depth repair work than most of our competitors.

I have a good relationship with my local competitors. Some buy parts from me because I have several dealerships. We stock a lot of parts and we order often. Competitors also send business my way when a customer needs something outside of the realm of what they offer. Some of my competitors only repair guitars and don't sell them or give lessons, so they refer people to AM Guitar Works if they need a new guitar or lessons. It pays to keep things friendly. After all, we're talking about guitars, music, peace and love, right?

Reconnaissance Missions

Something we do occasionally, either myself or an employee, is reconnaissance. We visit other guitar stores just to check them out. We do this locally, or when we are in other towns. We look to see how they compare to our business. We look for what we like about their shop or what we don't like. Here are some of the things we evaluate:

- First impression. When you walk in the door, check the appearance of the store. Is it clean and organized, or dirty and messy? I evaluate my location like this every morning when I walk in the door. Look at it from a customer perspective. What is going to be their first impression when they come to your shop?
- How are you greeted? If at all? Believe it or not, I have been to places where no one spoke to me, even when walking within a few feet from them.
- How are their sales associates? Do they seem knowledgeable? Are they properly dressed? I have seen store employees with pants around their thighs with their boxers showing. I know that's supposed to be cool, but there are a lot of people who are not going to be impressed by that. That type of dress really doesn't belong in retail. I'm not being judgmental. If that's how you like to wear your pants, fine, but not in a professional setting. I have also been to stores where the employees act as if you are bothering them by trying to make a purchase. I needed some knobs to finish a project quickly, so I went to a competitor to purchase them. I talked to the tech behind the counter because the knobs I needed were right behind him. He seemed annoyed that he had to interrupt what he was doing to reach up and get the knobs. I told him I would take them. He got on the intercom and said "Joe to accessories". (Name changed to protect the "not-so innocent".) When 'Joe' got to the counter he asked the tech "Who is supposed to be working accessories?" The tech said "Evidently you are". I don't know what

183

important project I took him away from. I was the only customer in the store. I wonder why that was.

- If I have a question, do they know the answer? If they don't, do they ask someone else or do they offer to find out and get back with me?
- When trying out guitars, how do they feel? Are they properly set up? Do they take care of their instruments?

Competition is something with which every business has to deal. Instead of fearing it, be competitive. Raise the bar in your chosen field and strive to do more and be better than your competitors. Dare to be different. Look for items and services to offer that your competition doesn't. Stay friendly with your competitors and don't badmouth them. They may refer business to you. Return the favor when applicable. By doing all this, you will improve your chances of success making money in the guitar biz.

Chapter 22
Taking the Leap From Employee to Self-Employed

I originally posted this as a blog post on Speak Out Small Business. It may repeat earlier parts of this book. Consider it a bonus chapter.

Is your dream to turn your hobby, passion, or part time business into a full time venture? Do you feel your "day job" is keeping you from achieving your personal goals? Do you dream of being your own boss and doing what you love for a living?

I was in this position six years ago. I had been with an office equipment company for 22 years, first as a technician, then as a manager. After being in the management position for 10 years, I started feeling like I was ready for something different. Guitar and music have always been my passion (obsession). It had been a life-long dream of mine to make my living with guitars. Not just playing, but owning a guitar shop.

Throughout my career I was giving guitar lessons, playing in bands, and doing repairs part time for extra money. One day I was visiting with some fellow guitar players and they were talking about how the guy who used to repair and customize everyone's guitars had moved out of the Quad Cities. I told them I did that type of work, and they started bringing me their guitars to repair. I had found a need that needed to be filled in this area. The wheels started turning. Was this my opportunity to follow my dream?

"The Dream Giver"

One day my wife came home from a women's conference with a CD of a presentation from the conference. She told me I HAD to listen to it. After a few weeks of ignoring her request, I finally (reluctantly) listened to it in the car on a business trip. Then I listened to it on the way home and several other times. The presentation was based on the book *The Dream Giver* by Bruce Wilkinson. I bought the book. The premise is everyone is born for a purpose and we are all given our dream at an early age. Hello? I had dreamed of making my living with guitars since about age 10. The book says most people never follow through with their dream because they get caught up in their day to day routines. This book pushed me over the edge to pursue my dream. I was 45 years old, working in a job that was stressing me out, but enjoying my part time venture. The book talks about what you will go through, both highs and lows. It's an easy read and I highly recommend the book to anyone who is considering following their dream.

The difference between a dream and a goal is a timeline, hard work, and an action plan.

In May of 2008, I officially launched my part time business, AM Guitar Repair, and set up a website with the help of a friend. I also invested in myself by taking a fretwork class in Chicago. This was an area I was not familiar with in guitar work. I made some business cards and went to a local lesson studio that started sending repairs to me. Then one of the large guitar shops started sending work to me. At this point, I was working a stressful day job, coming home and working until 10 at night and all weekend either giving lessons or doing repairs just to stay caught up.

Just a couple of months later, I was travelling to Minneapolis for a meeting. My wife, Julie, was with me so we had several hours to visit. I told her that I needed to make the guitar biz my full time job, or start turning business away. Fortunately, she was very supportive. In those few hours, we set a date. January 1, 2009 would be the goal date. There were several things that had to happen, and we started working toward that.

Besides confiding in my wife, I visited my good friend Dino Hayz who owns The Center for Living Arts. He was running a successful business and offered lots of suggestions. He was very encouraging and told me once you work for yourself, you never want to work for anyone else. How true that is!

I wrote a business plan that provided us with the same amount I was making as a manager. Since I was basically working two full time jobs, all the guitar money was going into a savings account so we would have a "cushion" when the paychecks stopped. What wasn't going into savings was being invested in the business. We had saved a few months pay by the time I left my employer.

A big obstacle we had to overcome was insurance benefits. My wife was working in a job she loved, but that year they cut her hours back by 15 minutes per day, making her part time and causing her to lose her benefits. We discussed that she would probably have to find a job with insurance if this was going to work. She said she loved her job and didn't want to do something she didn't love just so I could live my dream. I didn't want that for her either. She said God would have to "hit her upside the head to leave her job". I told her to brace herself because it was going to happen.

Long story short, she ended up with a job she loves, working for a university with great insurance benefits. As a bonus, my daughter is getting free college tuition there! All the pieces were fitting into place – even better than we could have imagined. We could see that this was meant to be. We are people of faith and it's as if God's hand was guiding us through the process.

December 2008 – The Longest Month Ever

At the end of November, I turned in my resignation with a 30 day notice . What was I thinking! I figured since I had been there for 22 years, I would give them time to transition. It was the longest month of my life. My heart was not in it. I was ready to get going on my new life as a business owner. I walked around the house saying "I quit my job." repeatedly at random times. Lesson learned – give two weeks' notice and let your employer deal with your leaving.

Self-Employment

Once I was able to put all my efforts into the business, it started growing. Owning a business is like having a child. You have to nurture it and watch it grow. It demands all your attention. You have to get it through the hard times. You have to expand what your business does to grow it and keep yourself from getting bored. We started out in the basement of our home. In 2010, the business moved to a commercial space in an old school building. We were hidden away with no outdoor signage. In late 2012 we moved to our current location which is near a busy intersection in a retail part of town. We have signage on a busy street that helps people find us. We changed the business name from AM Guitar Repair to AM Guitar Works and started carrying several lines of guitars and amplifiers that we sell.

My daughter, Brianna, now works for me part time. She is very creative and manages our store appearance and a lot of our social media posts. My son, Nick, gave drum lessons there as well, until he moved out of the area. This has been a good experience for my kids to learn about business and following their dreams as well.

In 2014 we hired another part time employee. This would be our first employee who was not a family member. She is one of my guitar students and has taken my guitar building class. She enjoys the guitar repair and maintenance part of the business and is a great help in that area. I can attribute decreased turnaround times and increased repair profits per month with the work she is doing.

We are reaching new goals, but the best is yet to come. As we say in the guitar business – Stay tuned…

Conclusion and Summary
I hope if you're thinking of making the leap from employee to self-employed, you follow through with it. It may seem risky, but many people have done it. With internet and social media there has never been a better time. It is inexpensive and easy to advertise. Just make sure if you are making the leap, you take the correct steps. My suggestions in a nutshell:

- If possible, start part-time and grow the business while you still have a paycheck.
- Read *The Dream Giver* by Bruce Wilkinson.
- Set up a website AND a Facebook page for your business

- Confide in your spouse, family, and friends. Talk to other business owners.
- Surround yourself with positive, supportive people.
- Write a business plan to make sure you are able to make the leap.
- Give yourself a goal date and a timeline when everything needs to happen.
- Take the steps you wrote down. Educate yourself on the things you're not familiar with.
- Throughout the process, save up money for a cushion when the paychecks stop.
- Give your employer your resignation. 2 weeks notice is sufficient.
- Follow your dream and watch it grow.
- Work hard, read, learn, network, pray, promote, and enjoy your business and your life!

Chapter 23
Using Your Powers for Good

The Merriam-Webster dictionary definition of **business**: the activity of making, buying, or selling goods in exchange for money.

This book has been about how to make money in the guitar biz. I hope that it benefits you and allows you to help pursue your dream. One thing I've learned is that it's not all about generating income for you, though that's a big part of it. A business or individual cannot exist without having money to pay the bills or feed your family.

I have been blessed to get up every morning and go do something I love every day. I also like to give back and there are many ways that can be done.

Mentoring
One of the purposes of this book, besides generating income for the author, is to mentor you, the reader. Since I opened AM Guitar Works, I have advised several people who are interested in owning their own business. I've been told that seeing my business grow was the inspiration for them to pursue their passion. It doesn't have to be guitar related. I've talked to photographers, cake artists, cookie bakers and more.

My experience has been that most successful small business owners are willing to give advice to other entrepreneurs or individuals wanting to start a business.

Hiring Team Members
By owning a business, you have the opportunity to hire people and mentor them. The positions I hire for at AM Guitar Works

are entry level positions. I pay an hourly entry level wage plus a commission on anything they sell. I also offer them the opportunity to teach lessons when they're ready. When teaching lessons, they are off the clock and making money as a music instructor.

One of the things I enjoy most about being a business owner is giving young people an opportunity to work in a job they are passionate about. They learn things that will benefit them for the rest of their lives. They see how a small business works. One of my team members has even started a photography business and is doing very well.

They learn sales, marketing, and administrative skills, instrument maintenance and repair, and how retail and online stores are built and managed.

They are also learning that helping others grow their musical talents by teaching lessons is rewarding, both personally and financially. They can make up to $40 per hour teaching. That's a very decent wage for a high school or college student.

They say to be successful, surround yourself with positive, talented people. My team members definitely fit that description. (I don't have employees. I have team members.)

Our business has grown and continues to grow thanks to their hard work and great attitudes. I do my best to make sure that they know what a difference they make at AM Guitar Works. I couldn't ask for a better group of people to work with.

Paying It Forward
From time to time, I like to contribute to a cause that helps people in need. Every fall we collect "Coats for Kids" at our shop. We take a big "Gator Cases" box and fill it with donations of new or used coats, hats, mittens and gloves. We hit up our

students and other customers to donate. For every coat donated, we put the donor's name in a jar. At the end of the collection period we draw out a name and they win a $25 gift certificate to AM Guitar Works. The winter apparel gets dropped off at a dry cleaner along with all the other donations from businesses and individuals. They are then distributed to people in need to help them stay warm.

There have been several people that my wife or I have known who have cancer. Many times there will be a benefit event. We have donated ukuleles with gift certificates as silent auction items.

We have also donated money and a guitar to Guitars for Vets. This is a great organization that provides guitars and lessons to veterans with Post Traumatic Stress. Look them up at www.guitars4vets.org

Our most recent donation is to The Will Foundation in China. The Will Foundation has taken in 11 orphans who could not be cared for at a regular orphanage. They range in age from 4-11 and are special needs kids. In China, there is a one child per family law. If a child is born with a birth defect, many parents send them away to an orphanage so they can have another "normal" child.

I learned of this group from a presentation at my church. A missionary from this area is going to be living at the house and acting as the teacher there. Among other subjects she will be teaching music. We donated six ukuleles and lessons for her so she can play for them, as well as teach them to play if they are interested. You can find information at www.willfound.org.

Marketing Opportunities
Paying it forward, besides contributing to a good cause, is also a marketing opportunity.

This can be a touchy subject because I don't want to make it appear that we donate to causes just so we can market ourselves. However, when you do publicize these things, it gives people a "warm fuzzy" and makes them want to do business with you. If you have more business coming in, that gives you more money to do good things.

The other advantage to publicizing it is that it draws peoples' attention to a worthy cause, and they may decide to support it as well.

Many times when you donate, you will get a "Thank You" card. Make sure you display that in your store.

The month that we donated those ukuleles, we had a record sales month for musical instruments. Some would call it karma. Some say that good things happen to good people. To me it just means that when we can bless others, we are blessed ourselves.

Chapter 24
Summary

When I started this book, I thought it would go fairly quickly. Fortunately, it took years to complete. My business grew during the writing of this book, which added more material for me to share with you.

I hope you found the information helpful and that you use some of the ideas in this book whether you just want to make some extra money or go into the business full time.

If you put the ideas in this book into action, you can make money. It takes hard work, lots of time and dedication. For me, though, it doesn't feel like work. I do what I love every day.

I would love to hear from you. Let me know what you got out of this book. What worked for you or didn't work? E-mail me at amguitars@mchsi.com with Guitar Biz in the subject line.

Sign up to "Like" AM Guitar Works on Facebook, follow us on Twitter, Pinterest, and Instagram to stay up to date with what goes on here and how we promote our business.

Good luck and have fun making money in the guitar biz!

Chapter 25

Resources

I have mentioned several times that this book is to get you started, but it does not have all the answers. Here are some of the resources I have used and found helpful.

Keep Up with Me
Websites:
www.amguitarworks.com
www.amguitarworks.highwire.com
www.reverb.com/shop/am-guitar-works
http://stores.ebay.com/AM-Guitar-Repair
www.guitarupgradesonline.com
Like "AM Guitar Works" on Facebook
Twitter: @AMGuitarWorks

Guitar and Amplifier Repair Resources
How To Make Your Electric Guitar Play Great by Dan Erlewine. An excellent book on setting up electric guitars. Includes a set of plastic radius gauges which come in handy.

The Guitar Player Repair Guide by Dan Erlewine

Dan Erlewine Repair Series DVD's – Available from Stewart MacDonald

The Tube Amp Book by Aspen Pittman - This is a great reference on how tubes and tube amps work. It's full of schematics as well.

"Tube Guitar Amplifier Servicing & Overhaul" DVD. Gerald Weber goes into great detail about how amplifiers work and how to service them.

Motivation and Business

The Dream Giver by Bruce Wilkinson - An inspirational book about following your dream. This one pushed me over the edge start my own business. Prepare yourself.

EntreLeadership by Dave Ramsey. A great book on being a leader and growing a successful business.

The Total Money Makeover by Dave Ramsey. Excellent financial advice for managing your personal finances. This is especially important when you are starting a business.

What You Gonna Do with That Duck? by Seth Godin. A collection of motivational writings taken from Seth's blog.

Purple Cow by Seth Godin - A book about daring to be different that contains many examples of businesses who stand out from the crowd.

Eat More Chikin: Inspire More People by S Truett Cathy. An autobiography of Chik Fila's founder. Find out how a child who grew up in poverty became the successful owner of a fast food chain.

Guitar Lessons by Bob Taylor. Bob Taylor tells the story of his career and the start and growth of Taylor Guitars.

Start: Punch Fear in the Face, Escape Average and Do Work that Matters by Jon Acuff. The title is self-explanatory.

Quitter: Closing the Gap Between Your Day Job & Your Dream Job by Jon Acuff. Another self-explanatory title.

The Complete Idiot's Guide to Owning and Operating A Retail Store by James E. Dion. A very comprehensive guide to starting and running a retail business. A "must read" if you are considering entering the retail realm.

Secrets of Closing the Sale by Zig Ziglar – An excellent book on sales techniques and strategies.

This is just a sampling of the resources I've used over the years to educate and motivate myself. Staying motivated is important when you are self-employed and growing a business. I could list, more, but find the ones that speak to you. Read and learn something every day.